Bangladesh's Road to Long-term Economic Prosperity

M. G. Quibria

Bangladesh's Road to Long-term Economic Prosperity

Risks and Challenges

palgrave
macmillan

M. G. Quibria
Department of Economics
Morgan State University
Baltimore, MD, USA

ISBN 978-3-030-11586-9 ISBN 978-3-030-11587-6 (eBook)
https://doi.org/10.1007/978-3-030-11587-6

Library of Congress Control Number: 2019931027

This Palgrave Pivot imprint is published by the registered company Springer Nature Switzerland AG
The registered company address is: Gewerbestrasse 11, 6330 Cham, Switzerland

In loving memory of my father, who gave me the greatest gift anyone could give another—he believed in me.

Preface and Acknowledgment

Since the founding of the country in the early 1970s, Bangladesh has gone through many ups and downs—economic crises and political meltdowns—instabilities that elicited widely divergent, often conflicting, opinions about its prospects. Once considered a basket case, it is now viewed by many as an inchoate economic miracle. This book is an attempt on my part to dissect and analyze the confounding dynamics of the country and examine the possibilities that lie ahead. In the process, I have identified some salient risks and challenges that may shroud the prospects of the economic and social transformation of the country.

This book grew out of a Distinguished Public Lecture that I was invited to give at BRAC University, a premier private university in Dhaka, Bangladesh, in January 2018. The lecture, captioned as "Reflections on Bangladesh Economy", was organized by the Economics and Social Sciences division of the University. The lecture was attended, among others, by the students, professors, professional economists, and journalists of the country. The positive response the lecture received from the audience was the main impetus behind revising and expanding the presentation into a book.

At BRAC University, Professor A.T.M. Nurul Amin, Chairman of the Department of Economics and Social Sciences, along with his colleagues Nilufa Yasmeen, Fahmida Saadia Rahman, and Farzana Munshi, bore the brunt of the responsibility for organizing the lecture. Also acknowledged is the warm hospitality of Professor Saad Andalib, Vice Chancellor of BRAC University, and Muhammad Musa, Executive Director of BRAC. All of the above also generously shared their views and insights on the economy of Bangladesh. The comments and observations I received from the audience during the lecture helped me to clarify my own perspectives and revise the lecture in important ways. I am particularly thankful to Nurul Islam, Fakhruddin Ahmed, Salim Rashid, Barket-e-Khuda, Albab Akanda, Syed Hasnath, Mohammad Zahid Hossain, Nurul Huda, Muhammad Masum, Sajed Rahman, Adil Khan, and Anis Chowdhury, who conscientiously read the various chapters in their preliminary formulations and provided much helpful advice and many suggestions. However, none of them bear any responsibility for any shortcomings and opinions, which are all mine.

I would also like to express my gratitude to various friends and Bangladeshi social scientists from whom I have benefited from discussions and exchanges over the years: A.K.M. Mannowar Uddin Ahmed, Ashraf Ahmed, Shamsun N. Ahmed, Syed M. Ahsan, S.M. Nurul Alam, Aminul Islam, Mian Bazle Hossain, Mirza Azizul Islam, Rizwanul Islam, Faridul Islam, Akhtar Hossain Khan, A. Rob Khan, Wahiduddin Mahmud, Raisul Awal Mahmood, S.R. Osmani, Atiqur Rahman, Zaidi Sattar and M.A. Taslim.

Anika Islam provided valuable assistance with graphics. Linda Loubert, chair of my department at Morgan State, provided encouragement and helpful logistical support to complete the project. Finally, I would like to thank Elizabeth Graber for commissioning the manuscript and for her help and encouragement throughout the process of preparing the book. At Palgrave Macmillan, Sujitha Shiney provided very helpful editorial comments and did an excellent job of editing the manuscript. Thanks are also due to Joseph Johnson and Allison Neuburger in editing and S. Sudha in production.

Finally, a large part of the credit for making this book happen goes to my wife and fellow economist, Shireen. Besides her valuable comments and encouragement, I could not have written it if she did not agree to take care of everything else. I should also mention our twin daughters, Naureen and Nasreen, who, despite their busy schedules and different professions, were willing to act as sounding boards for many of my ideas.

Baltimore, MD, USA M. G. Quibria

Contents

Abbreviations

ADB	Asian Development Bank
BADC	Bangladesh Agricultural Development Corporation
BB	Bangladesh Bank
BBS	Bangladesh Bureau of Statistics
BGMEA	Bangladesh Garment Manufacturers and Exporters Association
BIDA	Bangladesh Investment Development Authority
BMET	Bureau of Manpower, Employment and Training
BRAC	Bangladesh Rural Advancement Committee
CAR	Capital Adequacy Ratio
CPI	Consumer Price Index
CTG	Caretaker government
EPB	Export Promotion Bureau
EPZ	Export Processing Zone
EU	European Union
FAO	Food and Agriculture Organization of the United Nations
FCB	Foreign Commercial Banks
FDI	Foreign Direct Investment
FPMU	Food Planning and Monitoring Unit, Ministry of Food
FY	Fiscal Year
GCC	Gulf Cooperation Council
GDP	Gross Domestic Product
HDI	Human Development Index
HIES	Household income and expenditure survey
ICT	Information and communication technology
IFPRI	International Food Policy Research Institute
ILO	International Labor Organization
IMF	International Monetary Fund

IOM	International Organization for Migration
JICA	Japan International Cooperation Agency
LC	Letter of Credit
LFP	Labor Force Participation
LFS	Labor Force Survey
MPS	Monetary Policy Statement
NBR	National Board of Revenue
NGO	Nongovernmental organization
NPL	Nonperforming Loan
NSCs	National Savings Certificates
PCBs	Private Commercial Banks
PRC	People's Republic of China
PTA	Preferential Trade Agreement
REER	Real Effective Exchange Rate
RMG	Ready-Made Garments
SA	South Asia
SCBs	State-Owned Commercial Banks
SD	Supplementary Duty
SLR	Statutory Liquidity Requirement
SMEs	Small and Medium Enterprises
SOB	State-Owned Banks
UAE	United Arab Emirates
UK	United Kingdom
UN	United Nations
UNDP	United Nations Development Program
UNESCAP	United Nations Economic and Social Commission for Asia and Pacific
UNHCR	United Nations High Commission for Refugees
UNICEF	United Nations International Children's Emergency Fund
USA	United States of America
USAID	United States Agency for International Development
VAT	Value-Added Tax
WB	World Bank
WFP	World Food Program
WHO	World Health Organization

List of Figures

List of Tables

List of Boxes

CHAPTER 1

Introduction

Abstract This chapter begins with a thumbnail sketch of the state of economic development of the country at its founding in 1971. Since then, Bangladesh has made significant strides in economic development, which are reflected in its income growth, reduction in poverty, progress in various social and human indicators, and some improvements in infrastructure. In recent years, the country has recorded growth exceeding 7 percent. Impressive as this progress has been, this chapter posits that it would be hasty to conjecture that the future would be a replay of its past performance, given the various serious risks and challenges that confront the economy.

Keywords Famine • Poverty • Malthusian catastrophe • Social indicators

Bangladesh Then

Bangladesh became independent in December 1971 following a bloody war of liberation. Prior to independence, Bangladesh was one of the most impoverished and least developed countries in the world, having experienced little or no growth in its per capita income in the past two decades. Except for natural gas, it had no major mineral or natural resources; its factor endowments had been extremely unfavorable. In a geographical area of 55,000 square miles, the country housed 75 million people.

M. G. Quibria, *Bangladesh's Road to Long-term Economic Prosperity*, https://doi.org/10.1007/978-3-030-11587-6_1

Barring the city-states, Bangladesh was the most densely populated nation in the world—it had then 25 times as many people per square mile as the average of the United States, two and half times as many as that of the United Kingdom, and three times that of the average of India.

The situation worsened further with two major external shocks the economy suffered: one from the war of independence and the other from a colossal cyclone that preceded the war. The latter, known as the 1970 November Bhola cyclone, was the deadliest tropical cyclone in recorded history, which resulted in the deaths of up to half a million people (World Meteorological Organization 2017). It also destroyed or severely damaged hundreds of thousands of homes, fishing boats, and agricultural implements, along with most of the agricultural harvests of the country.

At independence, the vast majority of the people in Bangladesh lived in poverty and a large proportion of them in abject poverty.[1] This was reflected in a low per capita income, which was estimated to be less than $70 (in current prices at that time), and about 20 percent of the population subsisted on an annual income between $15 and $20. Nearly half of the population was severely malnourished, and more than 80 percent was suffering from some form of micronutrient deficiency.[2] Life expectancy at birth was about 49 years for males and 47 years for females. Child mortality was staggering, exceeding 140 per 1000, nearly seven times the average for developed countries at that time. Illiteracy was widespread—only 20 percent of the population was literate. At least 30 percent of the population was either unemployed or underemployed.

The housing situation was equally dire. For the vast majority of the people in rural areas, housing barely provided much-needed protection against nature. The urban situation was no better: about 70 percent of the population lived in temporary constructions that had little or no sanitary facilities, 80 percent lacked water connections, and 97 percent had no electricity. About 40 percent of the population in Dhaka lived in slums and squatter settlements (Hasnath 1977).

Agriculture was the primary source of income for the people, contributing 56 percent of gross domestic product (GDP) and providing 80 percent of employment. Though most of the people were employed in agriculture, the country did not produce enough food to feed itself. The juxtaposition of low productivity in agriculture and a rapidly expanding population led to increasing food deficits.

Compared with agriculture, the country had a relatively small manufacturing sector, dominated by large enterprises that contributed about

60 percent of its output; the lion's share of this output stemmed from jute processing. Thus, in pre-independence Bangladesh, manufacturing and jute processing were largely synonymous.

At independence, the state of physical infrastructure in the country was poor. Transport and communication infrastructure was woefully inadequate. The country had about 1800 miles of railroad, 2400 miles of paved road, and 5000 miles of river routes, which was then the dominant mode of internal transport. Access to electricity was very low—limited to a paltry 3 percent of the population. During the 1971 war, transport and communication suffered the most: most road and railroad bridges were either destroyed or damaged, as were a large proportion of the existing stock of trucks and buses. The two main ports of the country—Chittagong and Mongla—suffered significant damage during the war and were rendered dysfunctional for almost two years, with more than 40 sunken ships in Chittagong harbor alone.

At independence, the telecommunication system was extremely rudimentary, with minimal coverage. The damages the war inflicted on the network further weakened an already fragile communication system and severely impaired the government's capacity to run an efficient administration—including its ability to distribute food and agricultural inputs in the face of rising food shortages.

The war wreaked havoc with the rural economy. It not only destroyed or damaged much of the agricultural productive capacity—including draft animals, fishing boats and nets, and irrigation pumps and appliances—but also brought about a substantial depletion of the stocks of food, seeds, and agricultural inputs. To further exacerbate an already difficult situation, Bangladesh suffered a massive crop failure in 1972. The disruptions in the transport system, combined with the mix of adverse supply shocks in agriculture, created a condition of dire food scarcity in the second half of 1972. However, with the timely arrival of imported food from abroad, this crisis did not erupt into a runaway famine. Though this famine was momentarily averted, the specter of food shortages loomed large on the horizon. With continuing depletion of food stocks and another devastating flood in mid-1974, the country found itself engulfed in a massive famine in the second half of 1974. This famine resulted in the deaths of 1.5 million people.[3]

In the early years of its existence, Bangladesh looked like an absolute economic disaster. There was widespread concern, both within and without, regarding the viability of the economy. Bangladesh was widely seen as a Malthusian dystopia—a hopeless situation in which a mostly agricultural country cannot feed itself. A well-meaning authority on development from Cambridge University likened Bangladesh to "the textbook example of Malthusian stagnation", with little hope of escaping that impasse unless the population growth could be drastically reduced (Robinson 1973).[4]

The US State Department held a similarly pessimistic assessment of the prospects of Bangladesh. In the face of impending famine and social disorder, an official in the State Department, of which Henry Kissinger was the Secretary, derisively described Bangladesh as "an international basket case"—a country likely to be perennially dependent on foreign aid (US Department of State 1971).

Similarly, the World Bank was not too optimistic either, about the country's development prospects. Its first Country Director, Just Faaland, coauthored a book, *Bangladesh: The Test Case of Development*. In an otherwise sympathetic treatment, the subtitle took a not-too-subtle dig at the economy, on which they remarked: "If development can be made to succeed in Bangladesh, there can be little doubt that it could be made to succeed anywhere else. It is in this sense that Bangladesh is the test case for development" (Faaland and Parkinson 1976, 197).

However, as time has proven, the doomsday predictions for the Bangladesh economy were utterly premature. This event has also brought to the fore a much-overlooked fact that linear thinking in economic development, merely extrapolating past performance into the future, can often be misleading.

Bangladesh Now[5]

Fast Forward to 2018

Although Bangladesh, with many challenges, is still a poor country, it has made great strides in economic and social transformation. In recent years, Bangladesh has emerged as one of the fastest-growing economies in the world. Since 2005, it has, on average, grown at a rate of higher than 6 percent, despite various external shocks such as recurrent natural disasters, food and fuel price hikes, and the Global Financial Crisis. This robust growth has been accompanied by remarkable improvements in various social and economic indicators of well-being.

Bangladesh is no longer the test case of development; it has already "managed to place its foot on the first rung of the ladder of development"

(Sachs 2005, 14). These improvements have been noted by the international community. In 2015, Bangladesh graduated from the low- to the lower-middle-income group, according to the World Bank's classification of countries.[6] This is no doubt a milestone for a poor country, once considered hopeless, in its development journey. In 2018, Bangladesh has become eligible for graduation from its status as a member of the Least Developed Countries (LDCs). However, the UN's LDC graduation process is rather complicated—a country has to pass two triennial reviews before it receives its eventual certification of graduation. For Bangladesh, the next two reviews are scheduled for 2021 and 2024.[7]

Bangladesh's economic success is mirrored in its remarkable progress in poverty reduction. At the beginning of this millennium, almost half the population lived in poverty, based on its national poverty line; in 2016, that percentage declined to about a quarter of the population. In addition to these national estimates, the World Bank uses an international poverty line of US $1.90 a day (at the 2011 PPP exchange rate) to calculate global poverty. According to that measure, the incidence of poverty in Bangladesh declined from about 35 percent in 2000 to about 15 percent in 2016.

When the country became independent, the threat of a Malthusian catastrophe was frighteningly real; many economists thought that Bangladesh's ability to control population would be its litmus test for economic viability. However, belying conventional theories and beliefs, Bangladesh experienced a significant and sustained decline in the fertility rate (the average number of births for each woman of childbearing age, defined as between 15 and 49) since independence. As Fig. 1.1 shows, the fertility rate has declined from about 7 in 1971 to about 2.1 in 2017, moving toward the replacement rate. In this regard, Bangladesh, beginning with a higher fertility rate in 1971, outperforms both India and Pakistan.

Bangladesh has also made significant strides in health and education. Life expectancy at birth is now 72, which is three years higher than that of India and of South Asia, and four years higher than the average for lower-middle income countries. For other indicators of health and education—such as infant mortality, child mortality, maternal deaths, infant immunization, and female literacy and stunting—the improvements have been remarkable and exceed those of its South Asian neighbors such as India and Pakistan, despite their higher incomes (see Table 1.1). On this point, the *Economist* observes:

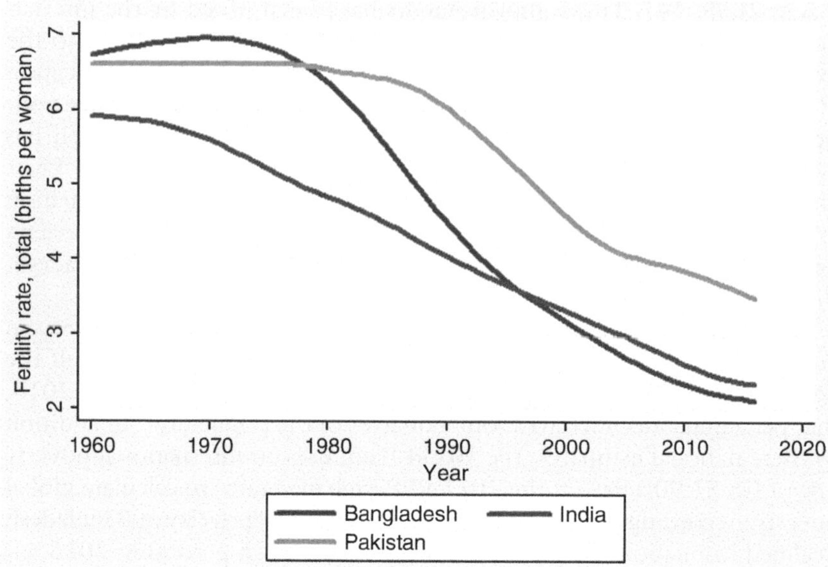

Fig. 1.1 Fertility decline in Bangladesh, India, and Pakistan over time. (Source: World Bank)

Table 1.1 Some selected health and education indicators: Bangladesh, India, and Pakistan

Indicators	*Year*	*Bangladesh*	*India*	*Pakistan*
Life expectancy at birth, years	2016	72	69	66
Infant mortality, per 1000 live births	2016	28	35	64
Child mortality, per 1000 live births	2016	34	43	79
Maternal mortality, per 100,000 live births	2016	176	174	178
Infant immunization rate, percent	2016	97	88	72
Female (aged 15–24) literacy rate	2016	94	82	66
Stunting, percent of children under 5	2016	36.4	38.7	45
Undernourishment, percent population	2015	15	15	20

Source: World Bank, World Development Indicators Database (World Bank 2018)

> The most dramatic period of improvement in human health in history is often taken to be that of late-19th-century Japan, during the remarkable modernization of the Meiji transition. Bangladesh's record on child and maternal mortality has been comparable in scale. (*Economist* 2012a)

Like India and Pakistan, Bangladesh is yet to achieve the goal of universal literacy, though it has made significant progress at the primary and secondary levels. The country's net enrollment rate at the primary level increased to about 98 percent in 2016 from 80 percent in 2000, and the net enrollment at the secondary level reached 57 percent in 2016 from 45 percent in 2000. Furthermore, the percentage of children completing primary school is now close to 80 percent. A remarkable aspect of this progress is that Bangladesh achieved this growth with gender parity in enrollment in both primary and secondary levels.

In some other health-related areas, progress has been mixed. Bangladesh enjoyed almost universal access to drinking water for many years, but this progress was set back when more than 20 percent of the tube wells were found contaminated by arsenic. In 2015, access to safe drinking water was restricted to about 56 percent of the population. Similarly, open defecation is virtually nonexistent in Bangladesh, having declined from 34 percent in 1996 to less than 1 percent of the population in 2015—thanks to government commitment, nongovernmental organizations' (NGO) efforts, and increasing rural income. This fact contrasts sharply with the situation in India, where 40 percent of the population—more than half a billion people—defecate openly. However, the quality of sanitation remains a concern as most of the toilets are still considered "non-hygienic".

In physical infrastructure, the country has made significant progress, even though major bottlenecks still exist. Road transportation is now the dominant mode. There has been rapid expansion of the road network since independence, with a road density of 166 (which measures the ratio of the length of the country's total road network to the country's land area), a statistic that compares favorably with the South Asian average.

Access to electricity improved gradually over the years. In 2016, it reached almost 63 percent, which is a significant improvement over the 3 percent at independence—although this still falls short of the average for South Asia.

Use of mobile phones has increased rapidly in recent years, reaching 78 subscriptions per 100 people in 2016. Although the increase has been phenomenal, it still falls short of the average for South Asia or the percentage of the lower-middle-income countries. Similarly, the use of the Internet was above 18 percent in 2016. Impressive as the number is, it still falls short of the average for South Asia or the average for the lower-middle-income countries.

Partly enabled by the rapidly expanding mobile technology, the country's performance in financial inclusion—meaning individuals and businesses having affordable access to formal financial services—has also improved. According to the Global Findex Database 2017, 50 percent of Bangladeshi adults had accounts in 2017, compared to 80 percent of adults in India, 74 percent in Sri Lanka, and 45 percent in Nepal, with the global average being 69 percent (World Bank 2017).

Bangladesh Tomorrow

What Does the Future Hold for Bangladesh?

Bangladesh has come a long way from a basket case or a test case of development to a (development) "standard for others to live up to" (*Economist* 2012b). In various social indicators, particularly in health and education, Bangladesh has set the standard for the developing world—its performance is deemed "exceptional", having surpassed those of other countries with comparable incomes.

The extraordinary resilience of the Bangladesh economy—from a state of hopelessness to bullish optimism—has attracted much international attention and has given rise to a good deal of speculation about its prospects. The assessments of the international development institutions are uniformly positive. A World Bank chief economist proclaimed that "With the right policies and a few timely actions, it is possible for Bangladesh to emerge as the next Asian Tiger" (World Bank 2015), which was further corroborated in Basu (2018).

Bangladesh has also become the subject of a great deal of international private financial sector analysis and speculation. Goldman Sachs has identified Bangladesh as part of its Next Eleven (N-11), economies that are likely to become, along with the BRICS countries, the world's largest economies in the twenty-first century (Goldman Sachs 2005). PricewaterhouseCoopers (PwC) projects that Bangladesh will be one of the top 50 large economies of the world in 2050 (ahead of Malaysia, Spain, Netherlands, and Argentina, among others) (PwC 2015).

Inspired by its recent economic success, the government of Bangladesh seeks to attain the status of a higher-middle-income country by 2031 and that of a high-income (developed) country by 2041. These are ambitious targets, achieving which will require further acceleration of growth on a sustained basis.

This study argues that linear thinking can be misleading as the future is not often a replay of the past. Notwithstanding its commendable economic and social achievements for almost two decades, the road to long-term economic prosperity may not be as smooth and rapid as it is widely presumed. There are many formidable risks and challenges that might decelerate as well as derail the current development trajectory. Those risks and challenges relate to changing external environments—such as changes in technology, rules of international economic engagement, and natural disasters and climate change—and the internal environment, reflecting various institutional and structural bottlenecks within the economy.

Organization of the Book

The second chapter starts with a brief outline of Bangladesh's political developments since independence. It is followed by an overview of the economic progress of the country in terms of growth and structural change. The final section of the chapter provides a brief comparison of the economic performances of Bangladesh and Vietnam to put the discussion in an international development perspective.

The third chapter highlights four serendipitous things that happened in the 1970s, mostly unforeseen by the economists and disconnected from the bloody political process of that time, that laid the foundation of the present Bangladesh economy. These relate to the emergence of the ready-made garment (RMG) industry, the start of international labor exports to the Middle East, the surge in agricultural growth, and the rise of NGOs.

The fourth chapter has two major sections. The first section highlights the major risks associated with the principal drivers of development in the economy. The first risk relates to technological progress—in particular, the ongoing technological revolution in robotics and artificial intelligence in manufacturing—which threatens to displace workers from labor-intensive manufacturing, such as RMG, and may bring about "premature deindustrialization" in newly industrializing nations (Rodrik 2016). The second risk relates to the prospects of labor migration as a strategy of development. The oil-rich economies in the Middle East are increasingly embracing the policies of Arabization in the face of falling oil prices and slowdown of their economies. The European Union countries as well as the United States are being seized by anti-immigrant sentiments and nativism. Those countries have been pressuring Bangladesh to encourage its unauthorized migrants to return, threatening to impose visa restrictions on Bangladeshi nationals unless the government acts to repatriate its citizens. The third risk relates to the agriculture sector, which has done a stupendous job of feeding the expanding population, but in which future expansion of agricultural productivity will depend on many factors, including the availability of further improved seeds and fertilizer technology. In addition, the agriculture sector remains subject to extreme vulnerability from climate change, particularly in areas affected by flooding, saline intrusion, and drought.

The second section of the fourth chapter discusses various social, political, and institutional challenges facing the economy. Those challenges include inadequate physical infrastructure, poor governance, skill and educational bottlenecks, demographic burden, dwindling social capital, and lack of transformational leadership, among others.

The final chapter strings together the major conclusions of the study. It also provides some observations on political, social, and institutional challenges going forward. These relate to such factors as governance, political institutions, economic openness, industrial policy, labor market and human development policy, investments in physical infrastructure, and the role of leadership.

Qualifications and Caveats

The title of this book may suggest that it provides a quantitative prediction of the future course of the economy, which is not the intent of the book. This analysis is not based on a numerically calibrated model, whose gains in precision are often offset by sacrifices of real-world textures and important economic details. Nor is it based on a collation of a set of vague and blindly optimistic expectations, leading to purely subjective prognosis. On the other hand, the objective of this study is to provide a reasoned analysis of the probable future risks and challenges facing the economy, and how those risks and challenges might shape the country's trajectory of development. In doing so, it seeks to shed light on the nature of course corrections, in terms of policy reforms and institutional innovations, that might be needed to sustain the tempo of development.

Second, this book is pitched at an intelligent readership, which is interested in the economy of Bangladesh—or, more generally, in economic development issues facing other poor countries at a similar stage of development—but not exclusively at economists with formal training in the discipline. It tries to avoid economic jargon and presents the analysis in a language that is accessible to people from a wide variety of academic backgrounds.

Nevertheless, as this study concerns economic development, it makes use of data and economic arguments to support its hypothesis. However, we believe even readers without formal training in economics would be able to go through those sections of the book, if they are not daunted by numbers and are willing to work through them with some patience.

Third, to analyze and describe what had happened in Bangladesh, one needs to rely on Bangladesh national accounts and other data, provided by the government statistical agency. Although some of the data are considered of doubtful accuracy, this is a problem endemic to most developing countries. Thus, these data need to be evaluated carefully and any data with spurious accuracy need to be discounted. The statistical outfits of international organizations such as the World Bank, Asian Development Bank, International Monetary Fund, and United Nations provide some scrutiny—although such scrutiny is far from comprehensive—before reporting them in their databases. This study makes use of data from both national and international sources, based on the author's assessment regarding their accuracy.

Notes

1. This section on the economic and social conditions in Bangladesh at independence draws extensively from the excellent account of Nurul Islam (1974), a leading development economist and the first planning chief of Bangladesh. The data cited herein are drawn from his work unless otherwise stated. Also informative is the analysis of Robinson (1974) as well as Robinson (1973).
2. Micronutrient deficiency relates to inadequacy in essential vitamins and minerals. It is a pervasive problem in many developing countries.
3. For an authoritative account of the 1974 Bangladesh Famine, see Islam (2003). Islam attributed the cause of this famine to a multitude of factors—both domestic as well as international, both economic and noneconomic. These factors include natural disasters, speculative behavior in the face of crop failures, adverse external macroeconomic circumstances, and nonavailability of food aid during the crisis. For a complex phenomenon such as famine, a single-factor explanation can be inadequate and highly misleading. In the Bangladesh case, international political–economic factors were as important as domestic factors. In the face of shortages in 1974, Bangladesh wanted to purchase food internationally from commercial sources, but could not do so as it failed to obtain the necessary commercial credit. In the meantime, US agreements to supply food aid under the PL 480 program were also delayed, mainly because US officials were negotiating in secret

whether Bangladesh should be debarred from receiving assistance as it had sold jute to Cuba, an embargoed country, earlier in the year. By the time American food arrived in Bangladesh in December 1974, the autumn famine was over (Rothschild 1976).

4. On this point, Robinson (1973, 46) mused: "'Is Bangladesh viable?' To that question, an economist has no answer. What is the alternative to viability? Death? Has any country ever died? It can be poor. It can be static. However, can a state not be viable?"
5. Unless otherwise indicated, the data cited in this section are drawn from the World Development Indicators of the World Bank.
6. The World Bank divides economies into four income groupings: low, lower-middle, upper-middle, and high. Income is measured by gross national income (GNI) per capita, in US dollars, converted from local currency using the World Bank Atlas method. Estimates of GNI are obtained from economists in World Bank country units; and the size of the population is estimated by World Bank demographers from a variety of sources, including the UN's biennial publication *World Population Prospects* (World Bank n.d.).
7. The UN classifies a country as an LDC based on three criteria: per capita gross national income (GNI), human assets, and economic vulnerability to external shocks. The latter two are measured by two indices: the human assets index and the economic vulnerability index. Income criterion is based on a three-year average estimate of GNI per capita. Human Assets Index is based on indicators of nutrition, health, and education. The economic vulnerability index is based on a whole host of different indicators such as population size; remoteness; merchandise export concentration; share of agriculture, forestry, and fisheries; share of the population in low-elevated coastal zones; instability of exports of goods and services; victims of natural disasters; and instability of agricultural production. To become eligible for graduation, a country must reach threshold levels for graduation for at least two of the aforementioned three criteria, or its GNI per capita must exceed at least twice the threshold level and the likelihood that the level of GNI per capita is sustainable must be deemed high (UN-OHRLLS 2018).

References

Basu, Kaushik. 2018. Why Is Bangladesh Booming? *Project Syndicate*, April 23. https://www.project-syndicate.org/commentary/bangladesh-sources-of-economic-growth-by-kaushik-basu-2018-04. Accessed 18 May 2018.

Economist. 2012a. Bangladesh and Development: The Path Through the Fields. November 3. https://www.economist.com/briefing/2012/11/03/the-path-through-the-fields. Accessed 12 Sept 2017.

———. 2012b. Out of the Basket. November 3. https://www.economist.com/news/leaders/21565627-lessons-achievements%E2%80%94yes-really-achievements%E2%80%94-bangladesh-out-basket. Accessed 1 June 2018.

Faaland, Just, and John Parkinson. 1976. *Bangladesh: The Test Case of Development*. London: C. Hurst and Co.

Goldman Sachs. 2005. Global Economics Paper No: 134. GS Global Economic Website, December 1. http://www.goldmansachs.com/our-thinking/archive/archive-pdfs/how-solid.pdf. Accessed 28 May 2018.

Hasnath, Syed. 1977. Consequences of Squatter Removal. *Ekistics* 198–201. JSTOR, JSTOR. www.jstor.org/stable/43618917

Islam, Nurul. 1974. The State and Prospects of the Bangladesh Economy. In *The Economic Development of Bangladesh Within a Socialist Framework*, ed. Keith Griffin and E.A.G. Robinson, 1–15. London: Palgrave Macmillan.

———. 2003. *Making of a Nation Bangladesh: An Economist's Tale*. Dhaka: The University Press Ltd.

PwC. 2015. The World in 2050. *Economics*, February 2015. https://www.pwc.com/gx/en/issues/economy/the-world-in-2050.html. Accessed 28 May 2018.

Robinson, E.A.G. 1973. *Economic Prospects of Bangladesh*. London: Overseas Development Institute.

———. 1974. Introduction. In *Economic Development of Bangladesh Within a Socialist Framework*, ed. Keith Griffin and E.A.G. Robinson. London: Macmillan.

Rodrik, Dani. 2016. Premature Deindustrialization. *Journal of Economic Growth* 21 (1): 1–33.

Rothschild, Emma. 1976. Food Politics. *Foreign Affairs* 54: 285–307.

Sachs, Jeffrey. 2005. *The End of Poverty: Economic Possibilities of Our Time*. New York: Penguin Publishers.

UN-OHRLLS. 2018. Criteria for Identification and Graduation of LDCs. http://unohrlls.org/about-ldcs/criteria-for-ldcs/. Accessed 28 May 2018.

US Department of State. 1971. Foreign Relations of the United States, 1969–1976, Volume XI, South Asia Crisis, 1971. *Office of the Historian*, December 6. https://history.state.gov/historicaldocuments/frus1969-76v11/d235. Accessed 26 May 2018.

World Bank. 2015. *Press Release: Jobs Critical for Bangladesh Development-World Bank Chief Economist*. December 14. http://www.worldbank.org/en/news/press-release/2015/12/14/jobs-critical-bangladesh-development-world-bank-chief-economist. Accessed 6 June 2018.

———. 2017. *The Global Findex Database 2017*. Washington, DC: World Bank. https://globalfindex.worldbank.org/

———. 2018. *World Development Indicators*. https://data.worldbank.org/products/wdi. Accessed 7 June 2018.

———. n.d. *How Does the World Bank Classify Countries?* https://datahelpdesk.worldbank.org/knowledgebase/articles/378834-how-does-the-world-bank-classify-countries. Accessed 28 May 2018.

World Meteorological Organization. 2017. WMO Determines Highest Death Tolls from Tropical Cyclones, Tornadoes, Lightning and Hailstorms. May 18. https://public.wmo.int/en/media/press-release/wmo-determines-highest-death-tolls-from-tropical-cyclones-tornadoes-lightning. Accessed 23 May 2018.

CHAPTER 2

Political Developments and Economic Progress

Abstract This chapter starts with a brief outline of Bangladesh's political developments since independence. It is followed by an overview of the economic progress of the country in terms of growth and structural change. The final section of the chapter provides a brief comparison of the economic performances of Bangladesh and Vietnam to put the discussion in an international development perspective.

Keywords Growth and inequality • Macroeconomic development • Foreign aid and structural change

Introduction

It is well recognized that politics has an important bearing on the process of economic development. Political regimes, political institutions, political stability, and the quality of governance—all influence the pace of economic growth and its distributional outcomes. This chapter starts with a brief outline of Bangladesh's political developments since independence. It is followed by an overview of the economic progress of the country in terms of growth and structural change. By design, this overview is selective as it deals with only those aspects that are germane to the question of the country's long-term development, which is the focus of this study. We will provide a more in-depth treatment in later chapters of some specific issues—such as the emergence of ready-made garments (RMG), international labor

M. G. Quibria, *Bangladesh's Road to Long-term Economic Prosperity*, https://doi.org/10.1007/978-3-030-11587-6_2

migration and remittances, progress of agriculture, and the role of nongovernmental organizations. Finally, to put the discussion in an international development perspective, the chapter concludes with a brief comparison of the economic performance of Bangladesh and Vietnam.

Political Development

When Bangladesh became independent, it was widely believed that economics would be the Achilles' heel for the country, while politics would be relatively smooth going. There were both historic and cultural reasons for this optimism. Regarding politics, it was thought that democratic values were in the DNA of the people, as the birth of the country was the outcome of a bloody political struggle for democratic rights of its people. Also, Bangladesh has a historically pluralistic culture with a long tradition of argumentation and public debate, intellectual pluralism and cross-cultural interaction—a tradition it has in common with India (Sen 2005). Finally, with few cleavages of caste and social stratification, its people are largely ethnically and linguistically homogeneous, sharing widespread enthusiasm for polls and politics. Although the aforementioned conditions should be conducive to a flourishing democracy, things did not turn out as expected—hopes were dashed almost immediately after independence.

In December 1972, the country approved a new constitution and adopted a Westminster-type parliamentary democracy. The system created the office of a strong executive prime minister, a largely ceremonial presidency, and a unicameral parliament. However, within a couple of years, in June 1975, as political and economic troubles—including famines—engulfed the country, the parliamentary system was abandoned in favor of a one-party executive presidency. Subsequently, in August 1975, the president of the country, who led the nation to independence, was brutally assassinated, along with much of his family.

This tragic incident was followed by a rapid sequence of military coups and countercoups, leading to the establishment of the military rule that continued for the next 15 years (1975–1990). During this period, the country was ruled by two army generals: General Ziaur Rahman and General Hussain Muhammad Ershad. To legitimize their rules, they created a civilian veneer of their administrations through the formation of political parties and experimented with the presidential form of government. They also undertook a series of market-oriented reforms, such as liberalization of the domestic economy and privatization of state-owned enterprises, and development programs, such as investments in physical and social infrastructure, which helped to put the economy back on track. Even though they were able to create a semblance of stability in the economy, both these regimes were rocked with occasional rebellions within the armed forces (General Zia was killed on the 21st recorded coup attempt by the military).

In 1991, a popular mass movement led to the reestablishment of the parliamentary form of government. However, this did little to improve the quality of political governance—it only shifted the arc of power from the president to the prime minister, who was anointed with the unchecked power of an authoritarian president. As if this was not enough, this enormous power of the executive was further bolstered by successive governments, which went on to curtail civil, political, and human rights by allowing arbitrary arrests, unlawful deprivation of life, regulation of speech, and weakening of labor rights. With few checks and balances in the system, the form of government that emerged was anything but a liberal democracy.[1]

Since 1991, the government became a duopoly of two major parties—the Awami League (AL) and the Bangladesh Nationalist Party (BNP)—and the position of the prime minister of the country rotated between their two top leaders. The personal backgrounds of the leaders—one is the daughter of the father of the nation and the other the widow of a charismatic military general and later president—and the way they inherited the mantle of leadership had had a tremendous impact on the dynamics of the post-1990 politics of Bangladesh. Their dynastic ascendance to leadership, without much political competition, largely shaped the way they ran their respective parties—much like a family business without internal democracy[2]; similarly, their personal backgrounds—once housewives, later accidental leaders—explain why political debates between parties often devolved into contentious issues of political legacies that had little bearing on important economic and social challenges of the country. The silver lining of this state of politics, if any, was that major economic policies were devised not in Dhaka, through reasoned discussions of merits and demerits by the political leaders, but in distant capitals where international development finance institutions were located.[3] This is not to say that politicians had been equally aloof about investment projects financed by donors; they bickered intensely over the financial spoils arising out of these projects. Like in many developing countries, the association between politics and foreign aid was far from benign (Quibria 2017).

An even darker side of this political duopoly was that, when in power, both parties tried their best to manipulate elections and exclude the other from political power. To create what was perceived as a level playing field, the country, with the consent of both parties, introduced a system of an interim neutral administration (Caretaker Government) to conduct parliamentary elections since 1996[4]; this arrangement, which had brought some level of accountability in a largely unaccountable system, was abolished in June 2011 with an amendment to the constitution.

In the absence of a neutral caretaker administration, apprehending widespread election rigging, the opposition BNP and its allied parties decided not to participate in the 2014 parliamentary election. For a country so besotted with polls and politics, the election garnered little voter participation—most parliamentary seats went unchallenged. The fate of the forthcoming parliamentary election, which is scheduled for 2018, remains uncertain at the time of this writing.

Since the inception of democracy in 1991, Bangladesh has made little or no advance in its quality of democracy—if not regressed.[5] At a very basic level, the broader democratic values or norms of a liberal democracy have not yet taken root among the political classes.[6] These norms are viewed as the soft guardrails of democracy that prevent political competition from spiraling into chaotic, no-holds-barred conflict. In the absence of such norms, the Bangladesh parliament has mostly ceased to perform its function as a legislative body: political parties seem more inclined to settle their issues in the streets than on the floors of the parliament—through street agitations and general strikes (i.e., shutting down of economic activities), coercion, extrajudicial killings, and riots. The adverse impact of the strikes on the economy—in damages and destruction of properties, loss of working hours, and business output—has been massive, let alone the potential economic damage from the negative perception they have on foreign investors.[7]

Besides the economic damage from the politics of confrontation, an illiberal democracy engenders other consequences for growth and distribution. The combination of an illiberal democracy (which affords limited accountability) with a fairly statist economy creates a toxic environment that inhibits free and fair competition, limiting economic opportunities only for those with direct and indirect access to political power. As expected, this has created a predatory political culture that thrives on economic rents extracted through discriminatory expropriation of state resources—or even flat-out thievery of state belongings. This pursuit of rent-seeking prevails at all levels from the top to the bottom of the political hierarchy and encompasses economic activities across the country, from metropolitan cities to remote villages.[8] Nor is the bureaucracy insulated from it. Recent years have seen increasing politicization[9] of the bureaucracy with party loyalists rewarded with accelerated promotions, lucrative postings, and important positions after retirement (Islam 2006). In a tradition of neutral and meritocratic bureaucracy, this trend has been highly disruptive. This unleashed fierce competition in the civil service for proving party loyalty rather than demonstrating merit; it also fractured the esprit de corps of the bureaucracy and introduced new elements of rent-seeking hitherto largely unknown to the system.

Besides the obvious efficiency and equity implications, the pernicious effect of rent-seeking on growth is well known in economics literature: it diverts talents from productive entrepreneurship to nonproductive rent-seeking activities and inhibits economic innovation.[10]

Economic Progress

Growth and Inequality

In the immediate aftermath of independence, growth was both slow and erratic, sometimes veering into the negative. War damages, natural disasters, and dysfunctional politics, all coalesced to keep growth constricted. Reconstruction and rehabilitation work took the entire 1970s, and it was only in the mid-1980s that the economy was restored to its pre-independence position (see Fig. 2.1). In the 1980s, the economy achieved a more stable growth rate that exceeded 3.5 percent. As the economy found its footing, the pace of growth further accelerated in the 1990s, averaging at about 5 percent. In the new millennium, with relatively more political stability, the economy saw a further acceleration in its pace of growth. In 2004, the rate of growth crossed the 6 percent threshold, a rate the country has maintained since then.[11] In 2016, the growth rate has surpassed the 7 percent benchmark. For a country that was teetering on the brink of economic insolvency a few decades ago, the current growth trajectory is impressive. Even more impressive is its achievements in many indicators of well-being, which are disproportionate to its income level, as described in the earlier chapter.

How does this growth performance compare with other Asian countries? In this connection, three observations are in order. First, notwith-

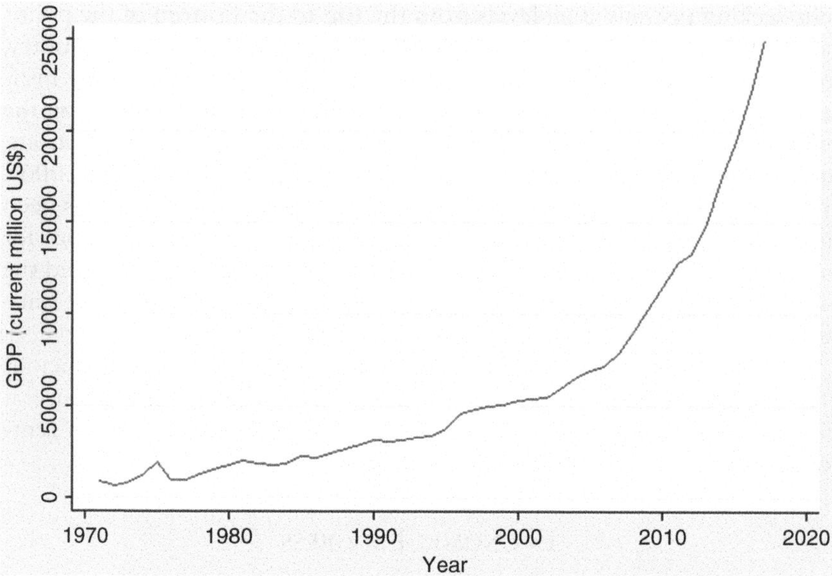

Fig. 2.1 Bangladesh GDP: 1971–2016. (Source: World Bank Data Indicators)

standing Bangladesh's recent success in generating rapid growth, it is premature to compare it with the economic performance of the East Asian miracle economies. It has yet to attain the ***depth and breadth***—implying the rate and duration—of the growth performance of the miracle economics.[12] Second, despite Bangladesh's recent growth surge, its ranking among South Asian countries, in terms of per capita income, has remained unchanged; the only two countries to lag Bangladesh are Nepal and Afghanistan—both countries are war-ravaged and still belong to the low-income group of the World Bank. Third, in developing Asia, those countries in Southeast Asia that were lagging or were at par with Bangladesh in the 1990s—such as Vietnam and Laos—have moved past Bangladesh.

Although the pace of economic growth is important, so is its quality—whether it is equalizing or not. The equity dimension of growth is captured by income inequality indices. One widely used indicator of inequality is the Gini index, which measures the deviation of the distribution of income (or consumption) among individuals (or households) within a country from a perfectly equal distribution. A value of 0 represents absolute equality while a value of 100 is absolute inequality. In Bangladesh,

Table 2.1 Trends in Gini index

Year	*Income Gini index*	*Consumption Gini index*
1991/92	38.8	27.6
1995/96	43.2	32.9
2000	47.2	33.4
2005	45.7	33.2
2010	45.8	33.2
2016	45.8	32.4

Source: Bangladesh Bureau of Statistics, HIES various issues

such Gini indices are obtained from the Household Income and Expenditure Surveys (HIES). The trends in income inequality and consumption inequality are shown in Table 2.1.

Table 2.1 shows that the income Gini index experienced a sharp increase in the 1990s, a trend which was somewhat arrested in the new millennium. On the other hand, the Gini index associated with the distribution of consumption expenditure exhibits a considerably lower degree of inequality. Although this divergence is confusing, it is not unusual for the two sets of estimates to differ. For example, for India, the estimate of income Gini index is also much higher than the corresponding consumption Gini index. According to a recent estimate by Chancel and Piketty (Chancel and Piketty 2017), the Indian income Gini index reached 50 in 2011 (which would make India one of the most unequal societies of the world), compared with the analogous estimate for the consumption Gini index of 36 in 2011. However, there may be a case for preferring consumption-based measures over income-based measures for two reasons: first, it is presumed that income data are subject to more measurement errors than consumption data; and second, consumption is a better indicator of individual welfare than income.[13]

To classify quality of growth, economists have used various labels such as pro-poor growth, inclusive growth, and so on. However, these concepts are not unambiguously defined. There are at least two measures of pro-poor growth in the development literature—an absolute measure and a relative measure. According to the absolute measure, growth is said to be pro-poor if the poor benefit in absolute terms, while according to the relative measure, growth is pro-poor if the poor benefit not only in absolute terms but also relatively more than the non-poor. The other term, inclusive growth, is used interchangeably with pro-poor growth in the absolute sense. Intuitively, growth is inclusive when all members of a society share the benefits of growth.[14] An examination of the growth incidence curves for Bangladesh—which indicate the growth rate in income or consumption between two points in time at each percentile of the distribution—suggests that the poor had benefitted from an increase in consumption in the absolute though not in the relative sense. This inclusivity in the growth pattern helps explain Bangladesh's past success in poverty reduction.

This inclusive growth was a silver lining in an otherwise bleak income distribution picture, which does not go well in a country with a very high aversion to income and wealth inequality—as reflected in its history as well as in the constitution that enshrines economic and social justice for all. In a milieu of dysfunctional politics and social polarization, this trend if continued might lead to serious political upheavals derailing the current development trajectory.

Macroeconomic Development

The role of macroeconomic stability in the process of economic development can hardly be overestimated.[15] It was most succinctly stated by the World Bank: "No economy can flourish in the midst of macroeconomic instability. Wild fluctuations in the price level, the exchange rate, the interest rate, or the tax burden serve as a major deterrent to private investment, the proximate driver of growth" (World Bank 2008, 53).

How has Bangladesh performed in terms of macroeconomic stability? Except for the initial years after independence, Bangladesh has performed fairly well. It maintained generally low fiscal and current account deficits, pursued prudent monetary policy and followed a competitive real exchange rate policy. Consequently, long-term inflation rate was kept to a single digit (there were occasional lapses, such as in 2008 and 2011, when inflation veered into double-digit territory).

This success in containing inflation was largely due to sensible monetary and fiscal policy followed by successive governments since the 1990s. The budget deficit was kept within prudential limits and a much larger part of it was financed externally. In 2017, the budget deficit had inched up and reached 3.5 percent of gross domestic product (GDP), of which 18 percent was to be financed externally and 82 percent domestically. In recent years, there has been a relative decline in the availability of foreign assistance, leading to an increase in the proportion of domestic financing, a policy that has direct bearing on the inflation rate.

The conduct of monetary policy by its country's central bank, Bangladesh Bank, was generally prudent. Broad money and domestic credit growth had been mostly within the planning targets set by the Bank. In recent years, private sector credit growth has been healthy, reaching around 17 percent in 2017. On the other hand, public sector borrowing from the banking sector has declined as the government has started to substitute bank borrowing by National Savings Certificates, a savings scheme for small savers; this policy leaves greater room for the private sector to borrow from the banks, but it also increases the costs of funds for the government as well as its future debt-servicing obligations.

The banking sector, which is the most important segment of the financial sector, is beset with many problems. There are three categories of commercial banks: state-owned, private, and foreign banks. In Bangladesh, as in most developing countries, there was over time a decline in the importance of state-owned banks, which tend to underperform in relation to other types of banks. From 2010, nonperforming loans (NPLs) of the banking sector have crept up and now exceed 10 percent of total loans. The share of NPLs is much higher in the state-owned banks relative to the other two types of bank.[16] In addition, some of those banks have failed to maintain the statutory risk-weighted capital requirements (Capital Adequacy Ratio, CAR). The poor performance of the state-owned banks in terms of NPLs and CARs has had an adverse effect on their profitability. All this requires the government to maintain a substantial budgetary provision for recapitalization.

An important reason for the poor performance of the state-owned banks, some of which were involved in outright fraud, is their weak governance. The boards of those banks were often chaired by political partisans rather than independent, qualified, and reputable professionals. Those chairmen could use the board as rubber stamps and make decisions that were often contrary to the interest of the bank. They took decisions with inadequate evaluation of loan applications and were involved in connected lending. To make matters worse, there were often no consequences for these unscrupulous activities. Not many board members or chairmen have ever been charged, let alone convicted.

In recent years, the country has maintained a modest current account surplus largely on the strength of workers' remittances. However, in 2017, there was a qualitative shift in the current account position; it turned deficit from surplus due to the confluence of a number of factors, such as the fall in export growth, the plunge in remittance income, and an increase in import growth. However, this adverse shock in the current account had been offset by the combined surplus in the capital and financial accounts, thereby increasing the gross foreign exchange reserve, equivalent to eight months of imports from the earlier seven months of imports. Foreign exchange reserves, while robust at the moment, could come under pressure if there was a decline or a reversal in current account inflows or a rise in various types of debt-servicing liabilities.

In this connection, two cautionary observations of the World Bank (2017) are worth heeding. First, Bangladesh Bank, the central bank, needs to monitor closely the liabilities originating from foreign loans taken by the private sector. The Bank should take a conservative stance in response to demands for partial capital account convertibility to allow Bangladeshi investors to invest abroad. Second, it would be prudent on the part of the government not to move forward on a proposal to create a "sovereign wealth fund" that would make the central bank's reserves available to finance large infrastructure investment projects. If this fund were to be launched, it could encumber reserves in a way that could negatively impact its resilience to external shocks or hamper the country's ability to tap global capital markets when required in the future. As the Bangladesh economy will continue to remain exposed to global uncertainties and external shocks, it is essential that the country's foreign exchange reserves be kept at a level sufficient to ensure the economy's resilience.

With respect to exchange rate management, Bangladesh Bank has done a reasonably good job. In general, Bangladesh experiences a higher rate of inflation compared to its trading partners, which would mean that Bangladesh depreciates its nominal exchange rate to maintain its export competitiveness. In the absence of such adjustments in the nominal exchange rate, the purchasing power parity theory would imply that the country will experience an appreciation in the real exchange rate and exports would lose their competitiveness. In recent years, Bangladesh has maintained a reasonably competitive exchange rate without any great swings in the nominal exchange rates. In 1917, however, the real effective exchange experienced some appreciation, despite the nominal depreciation of the currency against the US dollar. To preserve its competitiveness, Bangladesh needs to be on guard in case such a rising trend does get out of control.

Next, we briefly trace the developments of two major macroeconomic aggregates—savings and investment—and consider the role foreign aid played in filling the savings–investment gaps.

As expected, the rise in the pace of growth was accompanied by a rise in the investment rate. Starting from less than 10 percent of GDP in 1971, the rate of investment rose to about 17 percent in 1981. Since then, it has risen steadily to about 30 percent in 2017, a figure that is comparable to other South Asian countries such as India and Sri Lanka. This investment is comprised mostly of private investment, which rose from 10 percent of GDP in 1990 to about 23 percent of GDP in 2017. On the other hand, public investment (as a percentage of GDP) was largely stagnant during the decade.

Turning to the other side of the equation, savings followed a trend similar to investment. In the early years of independence, the country either dissaved or saved little. In those years, when domestic savings were negative, foreign aid had to be used to meet some consumption requirements. However, as the economy picked up pace, national savings increased and reached about 30 percent of GDP in 2016. However, a significant proportion of this saving, more than 5 percentage points, was contributed by overseas workers' remittances. In recent years, the savings rate went up further, reaching about 31 percent in 2017. This savings rate is comparable with India and Sri Lanka but ahead of that of Pakistan.

Thus, available data suggest that national savings run neck-to-neck with investment (while in some previous years, savings exceeded investment), implying that Bangladesh does not require any substantial foreign capital inflows to sustain its investment program. However, in practice, Bangladesh continues to receive a substantial volume of foreign assistance. This has to do with the fact that the government budget and development programs are substantially dependent on foreign finance, and so is the working of the country's large nongovernmental organization (NGO) sector.

Though the importance of foreign assistance is still high in the overall economy, its relative importance has diminished over time. In 1975, foreign aid accounted for about 90 percent of gross investment, which declined over time, reaching 40 percent in 1990 to less than 4 percent in 2016. Similarly, as a percentage of GDP, foreign aid came down from about 8 percent in 1977 to about 1 percent in 2016. Nevertheless, the absolute volume of foreign assistance received by the country did not decrease over the years (Fig. 2.2). The net amount of foreign assistance received by the country, however, showed substantial variability, fluctuating between 1 to 2 billion dollars between 1975 and 2011. In recent years, there has been an increase in foreign aid inflow, reaching around 2.5 billion in 2016.

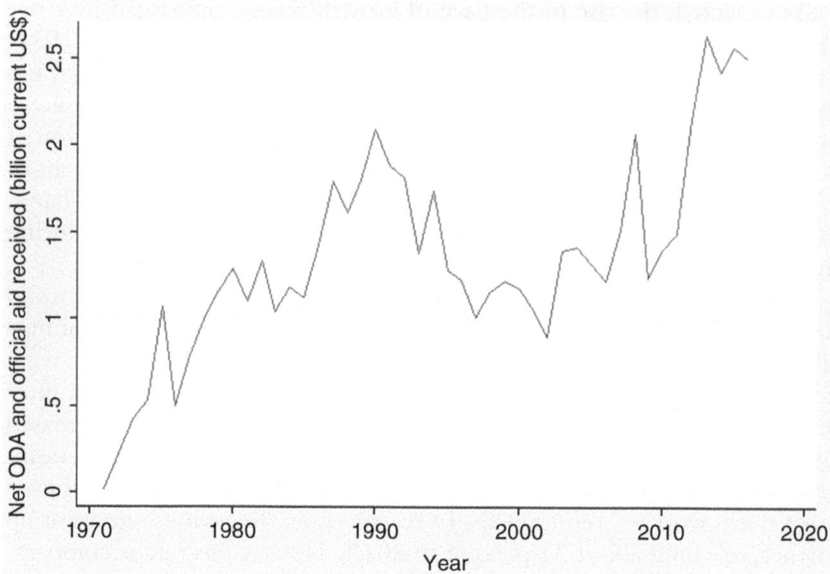

Fig. 2.2 Foreign aid inflow to Bangladesh (1971–2016). (Source: World Bank)

In this connection, three remarks are in order. First, even though the savings–investment gap has reduced, the government continues to rely substantially on foreign aid as it cannot mobilize enough resources domestically, either through taxation or borrowing, to fully fund its current budget or the development expenditures. This highlights the important fact that sufficient aggregate savings does not automatically translate into adequate investible resources for the government and a reduction in aid dependence. Second, in recent times, the country has seen a remarkable rise in foreign exchange reserves. This increase in foreign exchange reserve, despite a continued deficit in the trade balance, overlapped with a rise in remittances or a growth in capital and financial accounts, for example, disbursements of foreign aid.

Third, growth in Bangladesh was achieved without incurring a heavy debt burden. The stock of external debt has decreased from about 28 percent of GDP in 2000 to about 18 percent in 2016. This ratio is lower than the South Asian average or the average for the lower middle-income countries. In terms of the debt service burden, it amounted to about

5 percent (of exports of goods and services) in 2016, a figure that compares favorably in relation to South Asia, or lower-middle-income countries. The relatively low burden of external debt reflects the fact that Bangladesh largely shunned private borrowing and relied exclusively on either grants or concessional loans (loans with below-the-market interest rate and a long grace period). This shunning of foreign private capital stood Bangladesh in good stead: besides its higher costs, private foreign capital is often more volatile and can lead, in the context of a weak financial system, to the double mismatch of maturity and currency, and eventual financial crisis (Asian Development Bank 1999).

In contrast with Bangladesh, its South Asian neighbors, India, Pakistan, and Sri Lanka, relied more heavily on domestic debt to finance their government expenditures. During 1991–2005, interest payments in India, Pakistan, and Sri Lanka exceeded 5 percent of GDP compared with just little more than 1 percent in Bangladesh. During the same period, the three South Asian neighbors had to spend between 30 and 40 percent of government revenue on account of interest payments alone compared with only 13 percent in Bangladesh. This heavy burden of interest payments became a drag on the rate of public investment for those countries. However, of late, things have started to change to some extent in Bangladesh as well. In recent years, domestic debt financing in Bangladesh has been on the rise: in 2016, total public sector debt—comprising commercial banks' holdings of treasury instruments and nonbanks' holdings of national savings certificates as well as net credit by Bangladesh Bank and outstanding liabilities of state-owned enterprises to the banking system—amounted to 21.3 percent of GDP (IMF 2017). However, the debt service expenditure remains relatively low.

Finally, how important was foreign aid in the development process? Bangladesh has received more than $65 billion in foreign assistance since independence, which is a considerable amount of money, though not necessarily too large in relation to the country's overall requirements over the years. This assistance has been used in support of a whole gamut of activities: relief and reconstruction of the war-ravaged economy; building rural infrastructure (e.g., irrigation and rural roads); agricultural credit; urban infrastructure; transport connectivity; electric supply; water resource management, flood control, and drainage; skill and human resource development, including support for primary education and gender equity in schooling; health and family; governance; financial sector reform; and disaster management and climate change. Foreign assistance was not only extended to the government; it also played a role in private sector development and in funding the much-vaunted NGO activities of the country. It is well documented that not all foreign aid intervention was equally successful,[17] as many of these projects were botched by implementation delays, cost overruns, and other governance issues, including corruption (Quibria and Islam 2015). Nevertheless, there is no denying the fact that foreign assistance played an important catalytic role in Bangladesh's development process—it helped to create much of the physical and social infrastructure that was fundamental to its current social and economic progress.

Structural Change

Structural change refers to the movement of labor and other productive resources from low-productivity to high-productivity economic activities. The connection between economic structure and the level of development has been one of the most extensively explored themes in both historical and cross-sectional studies.[18] In one of the pioneering studies of structural transformation, Clark (1940) proposed a three-sector hypothesis of economic progress. According to this hypothesis, at the initial stage of development, economic activities and jobs are mostly based in the agricultural sector. With development, the share of agriculture in GDP decreases as economic activities and jobs shift toward the industrial sector, especially manufacturing. After a period of industrialization, the service sector gradually overtakes industry while the share of agriculture continues to decrease. In other words, at the final stage of development, people earn their livelihood predominantly from the service sector with a still important but diminished industrial sector.

In sum, the central thesis of these comparative studies is that for an economy to grow there must be structural transformation. This structural transformation can be evidenced from the patterns of growth which follow certain regularities, if one looks at one country at different points of time (time-series data), and at different countries at the same point of time (cross-sectional data).

The two most evident and used measures of structural transformation are employment shares and value-added shares of sectors in total employment and total value-added. Economists traditionally classify economic activities into three sectors: agriculture, industry, and services.[19] When the country became independent, most of the income and employment originated in agriculture. As economic growth picked up in the 1990s, the structure of production began going through noteworthy transformation. Prior to the turn of the century, both agriculture and industry contributed about one-quarter of GDP. At the turn of the century, the output share of industry began surpassing the share of agriculture. Its share in GDP went up to 30 percent as compared with agriculture's 15 percent in 2016.

Industry is a broad category; in addition to manufacturing, it encompasses a whole gamut of activities including construction, mining, and utilities. Over time, the share of manufacturing has gone up due to the emergence of the apparel industry. In 2016, manufacturing contributed about 18 percent of the output, which was higher than the contribution of agriculture. The share of manufacturing in GDP in Bangladesh now exceeds that of India or of Pakistan.

Since 1980, the most dominant sector has been services. This is the inevitable outcome of a set of push and pull factors: As rising population increased the burden of surplus labor in the agricultural sector, it led to an exodus from the sector, some of which was absorbed by the industrial sector; however, as the industrial sector was not expanding rapidly enough, some of the surplus labor was pushed into various informal sectors in the urban areas. Despite its expanding share of employment during the last four decades, the service sector, which is an amalgam of both high- and low-productivity activities, kept its share of GDP largely invariant at around 55 percent.

The current sectoral shares of employment are not in sync with the changes in the structure of production. Agriculture continues to employ the largest share of labor force, which is about 40 percent in 2017. Industry's share in total employment increased from around 10 percent in 1999 to 21 percent in 2017. With rising GDP, the share of construction (subsector) also increased correspondingly over the years. In manufacturing, textile and RMG is the major employer of workers, whose share had increased over time; leather and footwear has experienced a decline in their shares in total employment in recent years. The employment share of the services sector also increased from 25 percent in 1999 to about 40 percent in 2017. The transfer of labor that took place from agriculture went to both industry and services, but more to the latter than to the former.

This reallocation of workers between sectors had had a positive impact on real wages. As expected, rapid growth in manufacturing employment was accompanied by growth in real wages. Between 1980 and 2005, growth in real wages in manufacturing outpaced the growth in per capita income as well as growth in wages of all categories of workers. In a recent paper, Zhang et al. (2014) noted that since 2000, the country had a significant increase in rural real wages as well. They argued that this rise in real wages was due to expanding job opportunities in the nonfarm sector—especially for women in manufacturing—which was a major driving force behind the country's noteworthy success in poverty reduction.[20]

The main impetus of growth in manufacturing came from external demand. This growth was led by a surge in exports of RMG, which constituted more than 80 percent of exports in 2017. RMG has replaced jute goods as the prime export item, which contributed some 70 percent of all export earnings prior to 1980. The decline in the importance of jute goods was due largely to the advent of cheaper synthetic substitutes for jute products.

Over the years, the Bangladesh economy has become increasingly open.[21] This may be seen from various indicators of openness, including the trade/GDP ratio or the degree of trade liberalization. In 2017, Bangladesh's trade/GDP ratio had reached about 35 percent from less than 20 percent in 1990. To a large extent, this reflected the impact of significant reductions in import tariffs and in quantitative restrictions on imports. In the late 1980s, the tariff regime had become increasingly liberalized. In 1991 the average rate of tariff was around 70 percent, which went down to about 13 percent in 2013. Much of this reduction in protection was achieved by reducing the maximum rate. Also reduced was the number of tariff bands, which went from 24 in the 1980s to 18 in the early 1990s and to 4 in recent years. All these measures had simplified the tariff regime and helped streamline customs administration procedures. This reduction in the tariff rates during the 1990s also resulted in the decline in the import-weighted tariff rate, which fell from 42 percent in 1990 to around 13 percent around 2010. However, this reduction in custom duties had in recent years been offset by the introduction of a range of supplementary duties (SD) and regulatory duties (RD). In 2017, these para-tariffs (SDs and RDs) accounted for almost 50 percent of total nominal protection (Ahmed 2018).

Since 1990, Bangladesh experienced a healthy increase in exports, which grew at an average rate of 12.8 percent between 1990 and 2000, and at a rate of 13.4 percent between 2000 and 2017. However, this increase in export earnings was largely concentrated around RMG. Other export items such as footwear, leather products, and pharmaceuticals have emerged, but their contributions to export earnings remain insignificant in relation to the total pie. Most of these manufacturing products, which are geared to the domestic market, have not succeeded in creating quality jobs on a large scale. Some observers argue that this is in part due to uneven government policies that favored established and traditional products like RMG—which was provided with duty-free import of inputs, bonded warehousing facilities, back-to-back letters of credit (LCs), rapid custom clearance, and so on—and neglected nontraditional products that required similar forms of governmental assistance to enhance their competitiveness.

A Tale of Two Countries: Bangladesh and Vietnam

Like Bangladesh, Vietnam is an old country and a new nation. Like Bangladesh, it has a checkered history of political subjugation. Bangladesh was politically liberated in 1971, while Vietnam was liberated in 1975, marking the end of the almost two-decade-long Vietnam war. This paved the way for reunification of North with South Vietnam, and the establishment of the Socialist Republic of Vietnam.

In the 1970s, when the two countries started their economic journeys, they were both extremely poor and at the bottom of the economic pile of nations. Both countries are populous and highly disaster-prone. Vietnam and Bangladesh are ranked among the top countries likely to be most affected by climate change.[22]

Reform in Vietnam

Bangladesh initiated market-oriented reforms, along with privatization of its nationalized industries in the late 1970s while Vietnam began its economic reform program, known as *Doi Moi*—meaning renovation—to transform the central-planned economy to a regulated market economy in 1986.[23] Besides the extreme poverty and the highly agrarian nature of the country, the other factors that contributed to the urgency of this reform were the specter of poor economic growth, famine, large budget deficits, hyperinflation, a trade embargo from the United States, and drastic cuts in Soviet aid.

The reform program was comprehensive, cutting across all sectors of the economy. Prior to reform, agriculture in Vietnam was organized through collectives, which were particularly inefficient. The reform replaced collectives with household farms, where households received long-term leases with the right to exchange, transfer, lease, inherit, and mortgage lease rights. During the 1990s, there was further reform to relax restrictions on internal and external trade of agriculture goods—in particular, rice—and inputs such as fertilizer. The government also increased the quota on rice exports and removed restrictions on internal trade. Following the successful implementation of these reforms, there was a dramatic conversion of the Vietnam economy: it was transformed, from being a subsistence economy—perennially dependent on importation of rice—to a top exporter of rice.

Prior to *Doi Moi*, state-owned enterprises were the dominant means of production outside of agriculture. As in agriculture, the *Doi Moi* reforms introduced decentralized decision-making and gave enterprises autonomy over production, pricing, and trading. The government also implemented policies to introduce further competition by allowing the easy entry of private enterprises, including foreign-owned firms. Its foreign investment law of 1987 opened all sectors of the economy except defense to foreign investors; it allowed for 100 percent foreign ownership of firms, and offered foreign investors generous tax concessions and duty exemptions. Foreign investment was further encouraged by creating export-processing zones and industrial parks. These zones often offered firms reduced tax rates and exemptions on import and export duties. In addition, a number of other reforms were introduced to level the playing field among various types of enterprises—such as state-owned enterprise (SOEs), foreign enterprises, and private enterprises. These reforms include uniform rules of taxation, the freedom for enterprises to form their own trading relationships, and exposure to foreign competition.

Another important reform for the private sector has been the 2000 Enterprise Law, which made it easier for private enterprises to register and operate across most industries. This law, which reduced the time required to register an enterprise, led to the registration of thousands of new enterprises, following the enactment of the law. Most of the newly registered enterprises were privately owned firms. The new firms started operations in the enterprise sector, as opposed to in the household business sector, thereby helping formalization of the economy, which was beneficial to the firms, the workers, and the government. Formalization provides registered firms better access to markets and finance; it leads to higher wages for workers and a higher wage share in value-added; finally, it benefits the government by increasing the amount and the likelihood of tax payments (Boly 2015).

The rapid changes that took place in manufacturing in the form of expansion and formalization of private enterprises, restructuring of SOEs, inflows of new investment and technology, and improved incentive structures for production decisions: all have contributed to higher labor productivity in manufacturing.

Along with domestic reforms in agriculture and manufacturing, Vietnam undertook a program of extensive reform to open the economy in 1989. Prior to those reforms, foreign trade in Vietnam was subject to central decisions and was carried out by a small number of state trading monopolies. Exports were discouraged through the overvaluation of the exchange rate and the use of export duties; imports had to proceed through an extensive system of quotas and licenses; and exports had to fulfill partner obligations within the Council for Mutual Economic Assistance before they could be sold to the convertible currency area.[24] If those obstacles were not enough, Vietnam also faced a trade embargo with the United States that was lifted only in 1994.

The trade reform program of 1989 had to address a broad swathe of issues including: unifying and devaluing the exchange rate, relaxing import and export quotas, eliminating all budget subsidies for exports, simplifying licensing procedures for import and export shipments, and delisting items from export duties and reducing the rates for remaining products. In 1991, Vietnam allowed private enterprises to engage directly in international trade and, in 1995, removed all import-permit requirements for most remaining items.

These domestic reforms were quickly followed by international trade agreements and partnerships. In 1992, Vietnam signed a preferential trade agreement with the European Economic Community. In 1995, Vietnam became a member of the Association of Southeast Asian Nations (ASEAN) and its associated ASEAN Free Trade Area, which bound Vietnam to reduce tariffs on imports from ASEAN members to 5 percent or less by 2006 for the vast majority of goods. In December 2001, the US–Vietnam Bilateral Trade Agreement came into effect, leading to a huge increase in Vietnamese exports to the United States, predominantly in light manufacturing products. In 1995, Vietnam also initiated the application process to join the World Trade Organization (WTO) and won its membership in 2007. In addition to these, Vietnam had signed free-trade agreements with a number of countries or a group of countries, including Japan (2009), Chile (2011), Korea (2015), the European Union (2018), as well as the Comprehensive and Progressive Agreement for Trans-Pacific Partnership (2018). As part of ASEAN, it had been a signatory of a number of free-trade agreements with such countries as India, Australia and New Zealand, Korea, Japan, and China.

The policy of outward orientation of Vietnam played an important role in changing the structure of trade as well as in changing allocation of workers from agriculture (including aquaculture) to manufacturing, as agricultural exports became relatively less important over time. During 1997–2010, manufacturing employment grew at an average annual rate of 7.5 percent. Additionally, the liberalization of foreign investment and SOE reforms interacted in important ways with trade reforms and affected the composition of ownership of firms involved in international trade. By 2010, foreign-invested firms were responsible for more than 50 percent of all exports, compared with only about 25 percent of exports in 1995, while imports by foreign firms rose from 18 to 44 percent of total imports during the same period. Thus, Vietnam's trade reforms directly and in important ways impacted the structure of the workforce across firms of different ownership type.

The Great Divergence

The program in Vietnam, *Doi Moi*, encompassing privatization, liberalization, and international openness, had a dramatic impact on the growth and dynamism of the country. Between 1990 and 2000, the country grew at 7.9 percent annually, compared to 4.7 percent in Bangladesh. In the subsequent years, between 2000 and 2017, Vietnam grew at 6.3 percent compared with 6.0 percent in Bangladesh. These differentials in the pace of growth translated into significant differences in per capita incomes, although Bangladesh started with an advantage in 1990. In 1990, Vietnam had about one-third of the per capita income, in terms of current US dollars, of Bangladesh, but by 2017 Vietnam's income exceeded that of Bangladesh by more than 50 percent (see Fig. 2.3). A similar disparity existed if viewed in terms of purchasing-power-parity dollars.

The accomplishment of Vietnam in terms of poverty reduction was equally spectacular. The incidence of poverty, measured with reference to the international poverty line at $1.90 a day (2011 PPP dollars), was 2.6 percent in 2014 while the corresponding rate of poverty for Bangladesh was about 14 percent in 2016.

An important objective of the reform program was to open the economy to international trade and investment. From this objective, the program was a resounding success. The drastic reduction of tariffs as well as abolition of quotas and licenses in conjunction with a plethora of free-trade agreements catapulted the economy into an export powerhouse. In 1990, both Bangladesh and Vietnam had meager export earnings that hovered around $2 billion. Although Bangladesh exhibited robust export

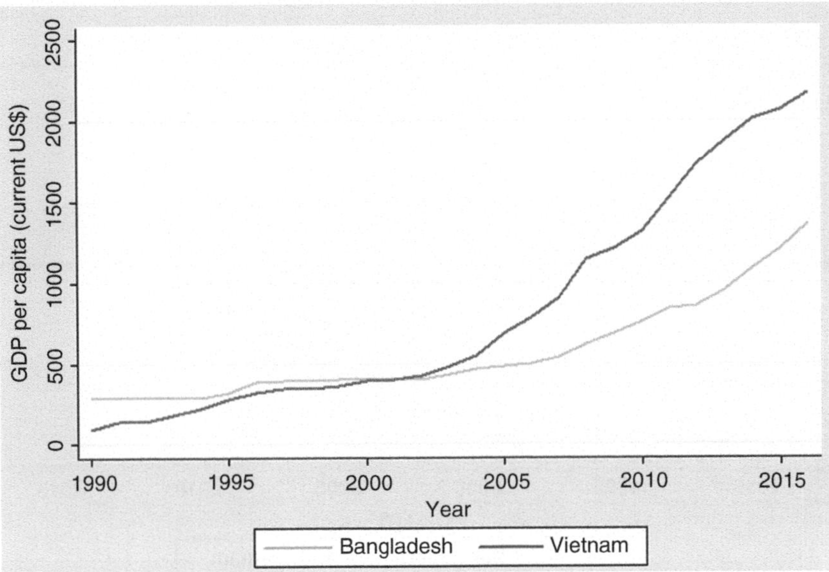

Fig. 2.3 GDP of Bangladesh and Vietnam (1990–2015). (Source: World Bank)

growth over time, its performance fell far short of that of Vietnam. In 2017, Bangladesh's export earnings reached around $38 billion whereas those of Vietnam crossed $227 billion, about six times that of Bangladesh (see Fig. 2.4).

The growing importance of trade in the economy can also be seen from the trade/GDP ratios of the two economies. In 2017, it was 200 for Vietnam while it was around 35 for Bangladesh.

An important dimension of trade relates to the composition of exports—the concentration of the export basket in terms of products. In the case of Bangladesh, the export basket has been concentered around RMG; on the other hand, Vietnam has over time remarkably diversified its economy in terms of both the range of goods produced and export partners. Vietnam now exports to a wider range of markets than ever before and has rapidly expanded exports in the manufacturing and electronics sectors, countering its once-heavy reliance on exporting agricultural products. Table 2.2 provides estimates of the concentration ratio of exports of the two countries. The concentration index, also named Herfindahl–Hirschman index,[25] is a measure of the degree of export concentration. An index value closer

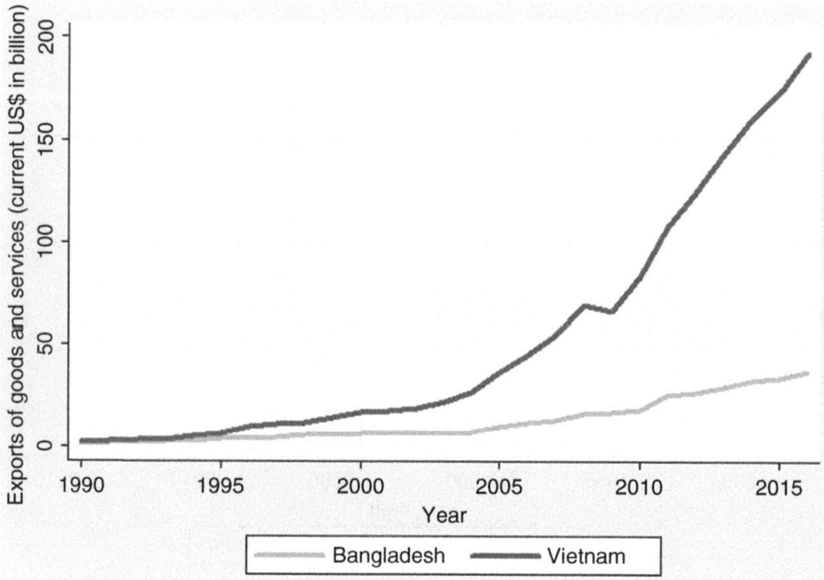

Fig. 2.4 Export earnings of Bangladesh and Vietnam (1990–2016). (Source: World Bank)

Table 2.2 Export concentration ratio

Year	*Bangladesh*	*Vietnam*
1995	0.336	0.200
2000	0.337	0.244
2005	0.388	0.226
2010	0.405	0.112
2016	0.406	0.191

Source: UNCTAD STAT (http://unctadstat.unctad.org/wds/TableViewer/tableView.aspx)

to 1 indicates a country's exports are highly concentrated on a few products. On the other hand, values closer to 0 indicate that exports are highly diversified across many products.

Using the 1992 revision of the Harmonized System (HS) classification, the diversity of Vietnam exports is also evident from the fact that the top exports of Vietnam in 2017 were broadcasting equipment ($34.1 billion);

integrated circuits ($14.9 billion); telephones ($9.9 billion); textile footwear ($7.94 billion), and computers ($6.36 billion). The corresponding list, using the same classification, for Bangladesh includes non-knit men's suits ($5.98 billion); knit t-shirts ($5.5 billion); knit sweaters ($4.47 billion); non-knit women's suits ($4.06 billion); and non-knit men's shirts ($2.5 billion). All the five items in Bangladesh top exports were related to RMG of various types (MIT Media Lab 2018).

Similarly, Vietnam was remarkably successful in attracting foreign direct investment (FDI). Prior to 1990, both Bangladesh and Vietnam received little FDI. However, since 1990, FDI inflows to Vietnam have been increasing by leaps and bounds, reaching $14 billion in 2017. On the other hand, the volume of FDI inflows to Bangladesh has been mostly tepid—not exceeding the $2 billion mark even in the best of recent years (see Fig. 2.5).

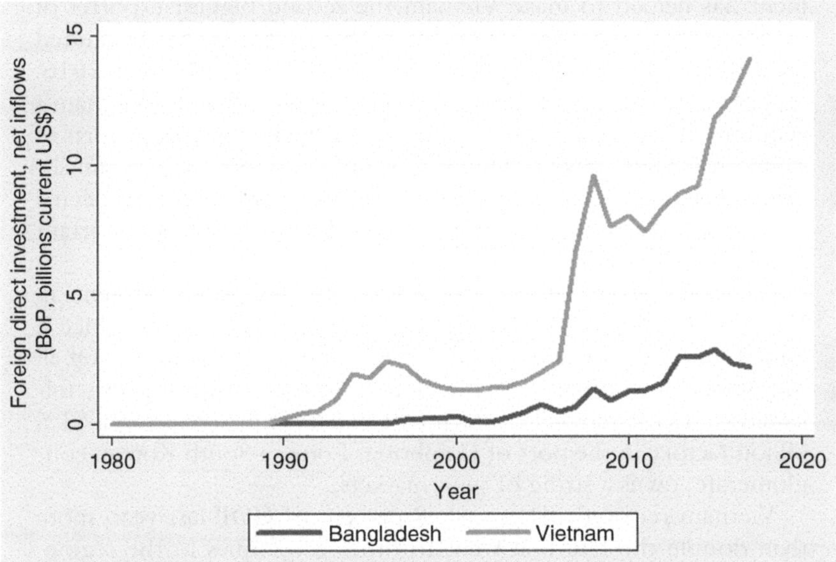

Fig. 2.5 Foreign direct investment in Bangladesh and Vietnam (1990–2017). (Source: World Bank)

Most FDIs in Vietnam came from South Korea, Singapore, Japan, and Taiwan, countries in which manufacturing costs are much higher than in Vietnam. FDI also played a critical role in changing the composition of exports of Vietnam. The share of high-tech goods in total exports from Vietnam went from 5 percent in 2010 to 25 percent in 2015 and has kept increasing with few signs of abating. Investments by electronics giants Hon Hai Precision, Intel, and Samsung—worth billions of dollars—have been instrumental in causing the shift in composition (see Box 2.1 for the role of Samsung in the growth and transformation of Vietnam). Electronics are replacing traditional manufactured products such as garments and shoes.

Box 2.1 Samsung in Vietnam

Samsung has invested a cumulative $17 billion in an electronics factory in Vietnam that employs more than 60,000 people. This investment has helped to make Vietnam the second-biggest exporter of smartphones in the world, after China. Samsung alone has accounted for almost a quarter of Vietnam's total exports of $214 billion 2016.

The Samsung investment has been a huge boon to Vietnam's economy. The Samsung factory has been a big magnet for all sorts of local businesses: new restaurants, shops, and hotels have mushroomed around this factory. In the last three years, there has been a sevenfold increase in the number of local firms listed as important suppliers to Samsung.

South Korea is the largest source of foreign investment in Vietnam. Of the $108 billion of FDI Vietnam has received since it joined the WTO in 2007, a third originated in South Korea. Of all the Korean investments in Vietnam, Samsung is the biggest, followed by LG Electronics, which makes television screens in a $1.5 billion factory in the port of Haiphong. Lotte, a South Korean conglomerate, owns a string of supermarkets.

Vietnam received FDI worth 8 percent of GDP last year, more than double the rate that went to other economies in the region. Foreign-owned firms now account for nearly 20 percent of the country's output. They have grown more than twice as fast as state-owned enterprises over the past decade.

For Samsung, Vietnam provides an attractive alternative venue to manufacturing in China. A principal attraction is its workforce,

(*continued*)

Box 2.1 (continued)
which is young, inexpensive, and plentiful. Compared to Vietnam, China's workers are now seven years older, on average, and more than twice as expensive as those in Vietnam. The cheap labor in Samsung's factories has helped to keep its costs down, giving it an edge over Apple in less expensive handsets.

Vietnam is also a valuable hedge against Chinese administrative caprice. In 2017, the Chinese government organized a boycott of South Korean firms and products to punish the South Korean government for its deployment of an American missile defense system. Although the system was intended to protect against an attack from North Korea, China complained it could be used to undermine China's defenses too. The boycott, although now over, alarmed South Korean investors.

Vietnam continues to liberalize its economy to attract foreign investments. In 2015, the government opened 50 industries to foreign competition and reduced regulation in hundreds more. In 2018, it sold a majority stake in the biggest state-owned brewer, Sabeco, to ThaiBev, a Thai beverage company. Vietnam's eagerness for free-trade deals has made it particularly appealing to foreign investors.

Source: *Economist* (2018): https://www.economist.com/asia/2018/04/12/why-samsung-of-south-korea-is-the-biggest-firm-in-vietnam (*Economist* 2018).

Vietnam's determined policy of openness to trade and investment has paved the way for significant gains in export competitiveness. Growing on the backbone of global value chains (GVCs), Vietnam has emerged as an Asian manufacturing powerhouse specializing in assembly functions by primarily foreign firms. According to the General Statistical Office of Vietnam (Government of Vietnam 2018), FDI accounted for 71.5 percent of total exports in 2016 (up from 47 percent in 2000), while the contribution from foreign companies toward the overall GDP increased to 18 percent from 13 percent over the same period. Many domestic electronics and automotive companies in Vietnam have also successfully integrated into GVCs. In general, Vietnam has emerged as an assembly platform, specializing in final production stages, including information and communications technology hardware and textiles and apparel, as well as a supplier of low-value-added intermediate inputs into GVCs.

The Vietnam government continues to focus on attracting FDIs, especially in sectors that facilitate technology transfer, increase skill sets in the labor market, and improve labor productivity to help it to move up the GVCs.

Concluding Remarks

Both Bangladesh and Vietnam experienced significant structural changes since the 1990s. However, from the perspective of pure structural change, the performances of both the countries are in many ways comparable (though from the pure metric of structural change, Bangladesh appears to be ahead of Vietnam in its transition to a service economy). Yet, Vietnam has had much greater success than Bangladesh in modernizing its economy, achieving both rapid growth and poverty reduction *à la* the East Asian miracle economies.

How does one explain the success of Vietnam? First, though Vietnam and Bangladesh both have the advantage of low wages and favorable demographics, Vietnam has leveraged its favorable demographics through effective investment in its people, which has included promoting access to quality primary education and ensuring minimum quality standards. Vietnam has a better educated workforce (90 percent literacy versus around 70 percent for Bangladesh) than Bangladesh. Vietnam is also politically stable and geographically close to major GVCs. However, this is not the central element of the story, which lies in its strong underpinning of good policies.

First, as described earlier, Vietnam embraced trade liberalization with a vengeance. These trade agreements brought about dramatic reductions in tariffs, helped lock difficult domestic reforms, and opened the economy to foreign investments. It is estimated that more than 10,000 foreign companies operate in Vietnam today, mostly in export-oriented, labor-intensive manufacturing (Eckardt et al. 2018).

Second, Vietnam complemented its program of external liberalization with its relentless pursuit of domestic reforms to enhance its international competitiveness and to improve the investment climate. This is reflected in such indices as the Global Competitiveness index 2018 (Vietnam ranks 55th, while Bangladesh ranks 99th among 137 countries) and the World Bank's *Ease of Doing Business* (World Bank 2018b), which ranks Vietnam 66th out of 190 countries on the ease of doing business—ahead of Indonesia (72), China (78), India (100), and Bangladesh (177).

Finally, Vietnam is at a relative vantage point compared to its comparator countries in infrastructure development. The country has invested heavily in infrastructure, especially in the power sector and trade connectivity. Vietnam spends 5.7 percent of GDP on infrastructure, compared to a meager 1.8 percent of GDP by Bangladesh. Vietnam invests the highest in Southeast Asia, which is ahead of India's 5.4 percent but short of China's 6.8 percent (Asian Development Bank 2017). Due to high public investment, the country was able to expand its capacity in power generation, transmission, and distribution to meet the rapidly growing demand of industrialization. Similarly, to keep pace with briskly growing container trade—which expanded at a staggering average annual rate of almost 13 percent between 2008 and 2016—Vietnam developed its connective infrastructure, particularly seaports and marine terminals (Eckardt et al. 2018). In overall trade logistics, Vietnam is far ahead of Bangladesh. According to a 2018 World Bank ranking of countries on trade logistics, Vietnam was placed at 39 vis-à-vis Bangladesh at 100 out of 160 countries (World Bank 2018a).

Notes

1. In his majestic account of the development of democracy, Stanford political scientist Francis Fukuyama argued that a flourishing liberal democracy needed to be built on three basic pillars: a capable state (meaning an effective and fair administration); rule of law; and government accountability (Fukuyama 2014). In Bangladesh today, as in many other developing countries, the quality of bureaucracy is weak. Although the country inherited a fairly honest and efficient bureaucracy and a neutral judiciary, its quality was gradually compromised with intense politicization by successive governments. In addition, in the postindependence period, both the bureaucracy and the judiciary suffered deterioration in educational quality and professional standards. This deterioration is reflected in the pervasive corruption that exists in much of the society today. With respect to the other dimensions of liberalism—that is, rule of law and government accountability—the country does not have as much of a strong tradition as India does. Both before and after independence, Bangladesh experienced successive regimes of authoritarianism which ruthlessly flouted these basic tenets of liberalism.
2. In his magnum opus, *Economy and Society*, German sociologist Max Weber defined patrimonialism to describe a ruler who regarded the country as "part of the ruler's personal household and private property" and ran the

administration along "purely personal connections, favors and privileges" (Weber 1978 (original publication, 1922)). Like many other third-world countries, Bangladesh today is a far cry from a liberal democracy—and it increasingly resembles patrimonial regimes of Weber.

3. For example, Brady and Spence (2010), which was part of the World Bank Growth Commission Report, noted in their preface that much of the market-oriented reform in the 1980s was conducted under the guidance of the World Bank and the International Monetary Fund. However, the outsourcing of major economic policies has not changed much ever since.
4. In 1990, Bangladesh introduced a system of neutral caretaker government to ensure free and fair elections without any political influence of the incumbent government. Initially established as a consensus among political parties, this system was formalized, in 1996, through a constitutional amendment. Under the caretaker system, the country was ruled by a non-political government for an interim period of 90 days during the transition from one political government to another.
5. The erosion in the quality of democracy is corroborated by recent assessments from various international think tanks. First, Germany's Bertlesmann Foundation, in its 2018 "Transformation Index", ranked 58 countries out of 129 developing countries as autocracies. Bangladesh, along with Lebanon, Mozambique, Nicaragua, and Uganda, was labelled under "new autocracies" (Bertelsmann Stiftung 2018). Second, Freedom House publishes an annual report, *Freedom in the World*, on the degree of democratic freedoms in nations; it provides an assessment of the current state of civil and political rights on a scale from 1 (most free) to 7 (least free). Freedom House ranked Bangladesh as "partly free", with a declining trend in aggregate freedom (Freedom House 2018). Third, the *Economist*'s Economic Intelligence Unit ranks counties on the basis of five categories: electoral process and pluralism, civil liberties, the functioning of government, political participation, and political culture. Based on this ranking, it divides countries into four broad categories: full democracy, flawed democracy, hybrid regime, and authoritarian regime. Bangladesh democracy was rated as a "hybrid regime", which ranks between a "flawed democracy" and an "authoritarian state". Its rank slipped 8 notches in 2018 from that in 2017. The position of India also slipped. It fell 10 places in the rankings from 32 to 42 (Economic Intelligence Unit 2018). Finally, press freedom is a sentinel in a democracy as well as an indicator of whether the democracy is healthy. According to the latest ordering of countries in press freedom, Bangladesh ranked 146 out 180 countries considered, which was below all countries in South Asia (Reporters Without Borders 2018).
6. It is well known that democratic institutions must be reinforced by strong informal norms and values. Democracies function at their best when such

unwritten rules of the game, known and respected by all players, ensure a minimum code of civility and cooperation.

7. According to a study by the United Nations Development Programme (UNDP) (2015), the costs of such street protests in Bangladesh in the 1990s were staggering, estimated between 3 and 4 percent of GDP. However, the frequency and virulence of these hartals have shown little signs of abating over the years.
8. A case in point is the public university. There is a close link between student politics, rent-seeking, and political violence in public universities. As noted by Suykens and Kutting (2018), there is a fierce competition on campus to prove one's bona fide as a party activist of the government, which needs the support of students to maintain its hold on power. Student leaders use interparty violence to show their commitment to the party and use intraparty violence to secure control of a faction. Such control—which signals capacities for violence and assertiveness—provides access to various opportunities: construction/procurement contracts within the university; a position in the student organization, which is often the stepping stone to an elected office or to the state bureaucracy—most specifically the police. These positions can be the gateway to middle-class lifestyles in Bangladesh.
9. Politicization refers to substitution of political criteria for merit-based criteria in the selection, retention, promotion, rewards, and disciplining of members of the civil service.
10. Murphy, Shleifer, and Vishny provided a theoretical treatment of the pernicious impact of rent-seeking on resource allocation and distribution. They argued that in countries with permissive legal systems and poor laws that permit easy corruption, high level of rent-seeking could be self-sustaining. This, in turn, could lead to a diversion of talents from productive innovation activities to rent-seeking and a reduction of growth (Murphy et al. 1993). Krueger (1974) wrote a seminal paper on rent-seeking in the context of development, and presented estimates of losses from rent-seeking in Turkey and India.
11. Year 2004 refers to FY2003-2004.
12. As the World Bank's Commission on Growth and Development (2008) noted, the high-performing East Asian economies—such as Japan, Korea, Hong Kong, Singapore, Taiwan, Malaysia, Thailand, and China—*all grew at a rate of 7 percent and above for three decades* before reaching their current stage of development.
13. It has been suggested that income is an unsatisfactory measure of individual welfare. Given the fact that income is often subject to transitory fluctuations, it provides a rationale for using observed consumption expenditures rather than income to estimate inequality. According to the permanent income hypothesis, differences in consumption expenditures

over time and between agents reflect differences in permanent disposable household income rather than transitory shocks to income. It is typically true that the distribution of consumption expenditures is less unequal than that of current income (Aitkinson and Bourguignon 2001).

14. The World Bank's Commission on Growth and Development (2008) associated inclusive growth with equity, equality of opportunity, and protection in market and employment transition. This is an elaborate definition that includes both the outcome and the means to achieve it.
15. In his review of the East Asian economic miracle economies, Quibria (2002) argued that macroeconomic stability was a necessary though not sufficient condition for sustained high investment and rapid growth. Until the 1980s, India had the macroeconomic stability of a "graveyard", yet in the absence of other complementary government policies and appropriate institutions, it could not achieve the kind of growth and poverty reduction that the East Asian miracle economies did.
16. The loan portfolios of even some of the better-managed state-owned banks have also deteriorated rapidly. According to a recent report, the bad loans of Janata Bank reached about 22 percent in June 2018 (*The Daily Star* 2018).
17. For example, a recent report of the World Bank on its Bangladesh investment confirms this mixed picture. It stated that "IEG (Independent Evaluation Group) has evaluated 16 operations that exited the portfolio during FY11-13; of these, the Padma bridge project was not rated (but with clearly an unsatisfactory experience). For the other 15 operations four were rated below the midpoint—all Moderately Unsatisfactory—and 11 above the midpoint including two Highly Satisfactory, three Satisfactory, and six Moderately Satisfactory. This means that 73.3 percent of the evaluated portfolio by numbers were Moderately Satisfactory and above—roughly the same as for the SAR region and the Bank's world-wide portfolio" (World Bank 2016).
18. The most notable among these studies include Clark (1940), Kuznets (1966), and Chenery and Syrquin (1975). They attempted to establish some stylized facts of development—that is, the patterns of development followed by most countries. A recent work of this genre, which includes a set of studies, is McMillan et al. (2017).
19. Bangladesh, which largely follows the international standard industrial classification (ISIC), divides its economic activities into three major categories: Agriculture consists of crops, livestock, forestry, and fishing; industry includes manufacturing, mining, utilities, construction, electricity, water, and gas; services correspond to wholesale and retail trade (including hotels and restaurants), transport, government, financial, and professional; and personal services such as education, health care, and real estate services.

20. Zhang et al. (2014) further argued that the Bangladesh economy had already reached the Lewis turning point, named after Nobel Prize-winner Sir Arthur Lewis. This refers to a development model advanced by Arthur Lewis, who highlighted the dual nature of a developing economy. The first component of the duality relates to its underdeveloped agricultural sector, which engages a major part of the labor force at subsistence wage; the second component of the duality relates to the modern market-oriented sector, which produces industrial goods at competitive wage. The growth of the economy is led by the modern sector with the support of the surplus supplies of labor drawn from agriculture. Finally, a point is reached when no more labor can be drawn from the agricultural sector at subsistence wage—and wages begin to rise. This is known as the Lewis turning point (Lewis 1954).
21. See Sattar and Ahmed (2012) for the challenges Bangladesh faces in diversifying its export basket, which is highly concentrated.
22. According to the Global Climate Risk index 2018, the list of top ten countries that were most affected by the impacts of weather-related loss events between 1997 and 2017 included both Bangladesh (ranked 6th) and Vietnam (ranked 8th) (German Watch 2018).
23. The narrative on reform in Vietnam draws heavily from Pavcnik and McCaig (2017).
24. Also known as COMECON, it was an economic organization that existed from 1949 to 1991 under the leadership of the Soviet Union. It comprised the countries of the Eastern Bloc along with a number of communist states elsewhere in the world. The primary impetus behind the establishment of COMECON was to foster greater economic cooperation between Russia and the weaker states of Central Europe, which were cut off from their traditional markets and suppliers in the rest of Europe.
25. The Herfindahl–Hirschman index is calculated by taking the square of export shares of all export categories in the market. The value of the index lies between 0 and 1.

References

Ahmed, Sadiq. 2018. The Political Economy of Trade Protection. In *Policy Insights*, ed. PRI (Policy Research Institute), 14–19. Dhaka: PRI. http://www.pri-bd.org/upload/file/publication/1536129694.pdf

Aitkinson, A.B., and F. Bourguignon. 2001. Income Distribution. In *International Encyclopedia of the Social & Behavioral Sciences*, ed. Neil J. Smelser and Paul B. Baltes, 7265–7271. New York: Elsevier.

Asian Development Bank. 1999. The Financial Crisis in Asia. In *Asian Development Outlook 1999*, ed. Asian Development Bank, 21–46. Manila: Asian Development Bank.

———. 2017. *Meeting Asia's Infrastructure Needs*. Research Report. Manila: Asian Development Bank.

Bertelsmann Stiftung. 2018. *Transformation Index BTI*. https://www.bti-project.org/en/home/. Accessed 27 July 2018.

Boly, Amadou. 2015. *On the Effects of Formalization on Taxes and Wages: Panel Evidence from Vietnam*. WIDER Working Paper 2015/042. Helsinki: UNU-WIDER.

Brady, David, and Michael Spence. 2010. *Leadership and Politics: A Perspective from the Commission on Growth and Development*, 1–17. Washington, DC: World Bank. https://openknowledge.worldbank.org/handle/10986/2404

Chancel, Lucas, and Thomas Piketty. 2017. *Indian Income Inequality, 1922–2015: From British Raj to Billionaire Raj?* WID.WORLD Working Paper Series No 2017/11. Paris: World Inequality Lab: Paris School of Economics.

Chenery, H.B., and M. Syrquin. 1975. *Patterns of Development, 1957–1970*. London: Oxford University Press.

Clark, Colin. 1940. *The Conditions of Economic Progress*. London: Macmillan.

Commission on Growth and Development. 2008. *The Growth Report: Strategies for Sustained Growth and Inclusive Development*. Washington, DC: World Bank.

Eckardt, Sebastian, Deepak Mishra, and Viet-Tuan Dinh. 2018. Vietnam's Manufacturing Miracle: Lessons for Developing Countries. *Brookings*, April 17. https://www.brookings.edu/blog/future-development/2018/04/17/vietnams-manufacturing-miracle-lessons-for-developing-countries/. Accessed 18 July 2018.

Economic Intelligence Unit. 2018. *Democracy Continues Its Disturbing Retreat*. January 31. https://www.economist.com/graphic-detail/2018/01/31/democracy-continues-its-disturbing-retreat. Accessed 10 June 2018.

Economist. 2018. Why Samsung of South Korea Is the Biggest Firm in Vietnam. April 12. https://www.economist.com/asia/2018/04/12/why-samsung-of-south-korea-is-the-biggest-firm-in-vietnam. Accessed 11 July 2018.

Freedom House. 2018. *Freedom in the World 2018: Democracy in Crisis*. https://freedomhouse.org/report/freedom-world/freedom-world-2018. Accessed 10 June 2018.

Fukuyama, Francis. 2014. *Political Order and Political Decay: From the Industrial Revolution to the Present Day*. New York: Farrar, Straus and Giroux.

German Watch. 9. *Global Climate Risk Index 2018*. https://germanwatch.org/de/startseite. November 2017. https://germanwatch.org/de/indizes. Accessed 23 July 2018.

Government of Vietnam. 2018. *General Statistical Office of Vietnam*. https://www.gso.gov.vn/Default_en.aspx?tabid=491. Accessed 18 July 2018.

IMF. 2017. *Bangladesh: Staff Report for the 2017 Article IV Consultation: Debt Sustainability Analysis.* Washington, DC: International Monetary Fund. https://www.imf.org/external/pubs/ft/dsa/pdf/2017/dsacr17147.pdf.

Islam, S. Aminul. 2006. The Predicament of Democratic Consolidation in Bangladesh. *Bangladesh e-Journal of Sociology* 3 (2): 4–31.

Krueger, Anne. 1974. The Political Economy of the Rent-Seeking Society. *American Economic Review* 64 (3): 291–303.

Kuznets, Simon. 1966. *Modern Economic Growth.* New Haven: Yale University Press.

Lewis, W. Arthur. 1954. Economic Development with Unlimited Supplies of Labor. *Manchester School of Economic and Social Studies* 22: 139–191.

McMillan, Margaret, Dani Rodrik, and Claudia Sepuleveda. 2017. *Structural Change, Fundamentals, and Growth: A Framework and Case Studies.* Washington, DC: IFPRI.

MIT Media Lab. 2018. OEC: Observatory of Economic Complexity. https://atlas.media.mit.edu/en/. Accessed 9 July 2018.

Murphy, K.M., A. Shleifer, and R.W. Vishny. 1993. Why Is Rent Seeking So Costly to Growth? *American Economic Review: Papers and Proceedings* 83: 409–414.

Pavcnik, Nina, and B. McCaig. 2017. Moving Out of Agriculture: Structural Change in Vietnam. In *Structural Change, Fundamentals, and Growth*, ed. M. McMillan, D. Rodrik, and C. Sepulveda, 81–124. Washington, DC: IFPRI.

Quibria, M.G. 2002. *Growth and Poverty: Lessons from the East Asian Miracle Revisited.* Research Paper Series, No:33. Tokyo: Asian Development Institute.

———. 2017. Foreign Aid and Corruption: Anti-Corruption Strategies Need Greater Alignment with the Objective of Aid Effectiveness. *Georgetown Journal of International Affairs* 18 (2): 10–17.

Quibria, M.G., and Anika L. Islam. 2015. A Case of Aid Effectives in Bangladesh: Development with Governance Challenges. In *Handbook on the Economics of Foreign Aid*, ed. Mak Arvin and Lew Byron, 429–455. Northampton: Edward Elgar Publishing.

Reporters Without Borders. 2018. *World Press Freedom Index 2018.* https://rsf.org/en/ranking. Accessed 23 July 2018.

Sattar, Zaidi, and Sadiq Ahmed. 2012. *Reducing Vulnerability in Export Performance.* Working Paper. London: International Growth Centre, London School of Economics.

Sen, Amartya. 2005. *The Argumentative Indian: Writings on Indian History, Culture and Identity.* London: Penguin Books.

Suykens, Bert, and Julian Kutting. 2018. Violent Democracy in Bangladesh. February 14. http://politicalviolenceataglance.org/2018/02/14/violent-democracy-in-bangladesh/. Accessed 4 July 2018.

The Daily Star. 2018. Janata Going BASIC's way. October 12. https://www.thedailystar.net/frontpage/news/janata-going-basics-way-1646047. Accessed 28 October 2018.

United Nations Development Programme. 2015. *Beyond Hartals: Towards Democratic Dialogue in Bangladesh*. Dhaka: United Nations Development Programme.

Weber, Max. 1978 (Original Publication, 1922). *Economy and Society*. Berkeley: University of California Press.

World Bank. 2008. *The Growth Report: Strategies for Sustained Growth and Inclusive Development*. Washington, DC: World Bank on behalf of the Commission on Growth and Development. https://openknowledge.worldbank.org/handle/10986/6507

———. 2016. *Completion and Learning Report on Bangladesh*. IEG Report. Washington, DC: World Bank.

———. 2017. *Bangladesh Development Update: Towards More, Better and Inclusive Jobs*. Country Economic Outlook. Dhaka: World Bank.

———. 2018a. *Connecting to Compete 2018: Trade Logistics in the Global Economy*. Washington, DC: World Bank.

———. 2018b. *Doing Business*. Business Report. Washington, DC: World Bank.

Zhang, Xiaobo, Shahidur Rashid, Kaikaus Ahmad, and Akhter Ahmed. 2014. Escalation of Real Wages in Bangladesh: Is It the Beginning of Structural Transformation? *World Development* 64: 273–285.

CHAPTER 3

Drivers of Development

Abstract This chapter highlights four serendipitous things that happened in the 1970s, mostly unforeseen by the economists and disconnected from the bloody political process of that time, which laid the foundation of the present Bangladesh economy. These relate to the emergence of the ready-made garment industry, the start of international labor exports to the Middle East, the surge in agricultural growth, and the rise of nongovernmental organizations. Notwithstanding various challenges, these four drivers of development have remained robust to this day and have contributed to the country's economic and social progress.

Keywords Ready-made garments • International labor migration and remittances • Agriculture and nongovernmental organizations

Introduction

The 1970s were in some sense the worst of times for Bangladesh. During this decade, Bangladesh suffered the worst famine and the deadliest natural disaster in recent history. It was also the time when the country was caught in "a legacy of blood", with coups and countercoups resulting in thousands of deaths—including the brutal assassination of the father of the nation. Also killed at the turn of the decade was the charismatic military general and later president, Ziaur Rahman (Mascarenhas 1986).

M. G. Quibria, *Bangladesh's Road to Long-term Economic Prosperity*, https://doi.org/10.1007/978-3-030-11587-6_3

In another sense, the 1970s also represented the best of times for Bangladesh. It was then that the country threw off its shackles and became politically independent. It was the time when the seeds of a quiet revolution for economic liberation—freedom from poverty and destitution—were sown. Though largely unanticipated by economists and mostly disconnected from the bloody power struggle that embroiled politics at that time, this quest for freedom from poverty was spurred by four serendipitous happenings that radically changed the course of the country's economic history. While politicians were busy tearing each other apart, masses of people—young females, impoverished farmers, unemployed youth, and destitute women—came out of the woodwork to join this movement to shape their own economic destiny. This evolving movement gradually helped to lay the foundations of what eventually emerged as the four drivers of the present-day Bangladesh economy.

First was the emergence of the ready-made garments (RMG) industry, which was pioneered by Noorul Quader Khan, a retired civil servant turned entrepreneur. In 1977, he set up the first export-oriented garment manufacturing factory, Desh Garments, which laid the foundation of a thriving garment industry that now constitutes the backbone of the country's export sector.

The second fortuitous thing that happened was, ironically, the oil crises of the 1970s that virtually upended the global economy and brought about a substantial redistribution of global income in favor of the oil-exporting Middle Eastern economies. With this new-found fortune, these economies decided to embark on ambitious plans of infrastructure building, which required importation of guest workers from other countries, given the relative shortage of workers in the Middle East. For many Asian countries, including Bangladesh, this created new earning opportunities, to which Bangladeshi workers responded zealously by moving to the Middle East in droves. Once the young workers became footloose, they gradually spread themselves to countries beyond the Middle East in search of new opportunities.

The third fortuitous thing that happened was the surge of agriculture. Immediately after independence, agricultural production tanked, leading to the worst famine in the history of the country. But since then, in the last 40 years or so, food production has soared—it more than tripled between 1972 and 2014. Rapid expansion of irrigation, improvement in rural infrastructure, liberalization of input and output markets—all this together created an incentive framework to which farmers responded enthusiastically.

The result was the rapid adoption of the new seed-fertilizer technology that brought about continuous increases in yields at an astounding rate.

The fourth occurrence was the emergence of a class of visionary social entrepreneurs such as Muhammad Yunus and Fazle Hasan Abed, who were gravely jolted by the mass sufferings that accompanied the war of liberation and the devastating famine of 1974 that followed. In their desire to make a difference, they went on to found nongovernmental organizations (NGOs), vehicles to experiment with their own visions of development. By doing so, they in turn helped to usher into the country an NGO movement, as many others followed. These social entrepreneurs pioneered many innovative social interventions, including the much-celebrated microcredit program that has been widely embraced internationally. These programs had a profound economic and social impact on the country, including a rapid improvement in social indicators of well-being, accomplishments that are now acclaimed globally.

The chapter is organized as follows: The next four sections provide a more in-depth discussion of the four drivers of development that kick-started the economy from its postindependence torpor; these four sections are followed by a conclusion.

Ready-made Garments

In the 1970s, the industrial landscape was rather desolate. This was succinctly described by Mushtaq Khan as follows:

> When Bangladesh became independent in 1971, there was hardly any Bengali-owned industry, and the little that had developed was destroyed by the sweeping nationalizations of the "socialist" regime. By 1974–5, the dominant economic organizations were public sector corporations that included almost the entire manufacturing and industrial base. The public sector corporations were largely inefficient and served as venues for job creation for the clients of the regime and enabled political accumulation based on price fixing, the political allocation of contracts and even outright theft. Bengali economic organizations in the private sector were for a while excluded from large-scale industry, and concentrated on trading and acquiring government contracts for infrastructure construction. (Khan 2013, 101)

In this milieu, the prospects of a thriving manufacturing industry seemed really far-fetched. Subsequently, when the ready-made garment (RMG) industry emerged and then thrived, it took most observers by surprise.

How a New Thriving Industry Was Born

In the late 1970s, when Noorul Quader Khan was contemplating an export-oriented garment factory, the domestic business conditions were pretty bleak. The linchpin of the manufacturing sector of the country, the jute industry, was in a death spiral for both supply and demand reasons. In the wake of the independence, this industry lost much of its production capacity as there was massive asset stripping in the public-sector jute mills; on the demand side, there was a precipitous decline in the international demand for jute goods due to the advent of synthetic substitutes.

As far as garment manufacturing was concerned, it was at a very rudimentary stage. In 1978, there were only nine export-oriented garment-manufacturing firms, whose aggregate export earnings did not exceed $1 million. Most of these units were small, producing more for domestic than export markets (Yunus and Yamagata 2012). The reason these firms did not succeed in making an international breakthrough was that they did not have what was required to succeed internationally—such as technology, management skills, and knowledge of international markets. Not having those skills, Noorul Khan was prompted to seek an international partnership that would provide him the missing ingredients for international success—that is, "the tacit knowledge"[1] for setting up the plant, managing quality control, minimizing wastage of raw materials, managing time and all the other aspects of factory production that determine the difference between profit and loss in a competitive world (Khan 2013).

A blessing in disguise for this start-up in an otherwise grim environment was the existence of international trading rules governing textile and clothing, a protectionist system codified by the Multifiber Arrangement (MFA; see Box 3.1), a quota regime that regulated the developing countries' exports to developed countries. But fortunately for Bangladesh, it was, like other poor countries, kept outside the purview of the MFA quota system, largely because it did not have much of a garment industry to pose a threat to the textile and clothing sector of developed countries.

In the late 1970s, garment exporters in Korea and elsewhere were seriously quota-constrained and were actively seeking collaboration with garment manufacturers from other countries that did not reach their quota limits (Rhee 1990). One such Korean garment exporter was Daewoo,

Box 3.1 MFA and Bangladesh

International trade of apparel and textiles has been subject to trade restrictions for a long time. As early as 1935, Japan was forced to announce its voluntary export restraint on textile exports to the US. Beginning with Japan's entry into the GATT in 1955, special trading rules were introduced to deal with potentially disruptive imports in clothing and textile products. These measures were first introduced as the Short-Term Arrangement covering cotton textiles (1961), then extended into the Long-Term Arrangement (1962–73), and finally incorporated into the Multifiber Arrangement (MFA) (1974–94). These agreements managed global textiles and apparel trade through a complex system of quantitative restrictions and voluntary export restraints. The products covered by these agreements thus were outside the purview of the GATT system of rules, disciplines, and enforcement. Under the MFA quota system, the exporter was allowed to supply a certain volume of textile and clothing products up to a specified ceiling—and it was up to the exporter to allocate the quota allowance among its domestic producers.

Since 1974, the MFA has been renegotiated four times and each modification has brought in its wake increasingly restrictive measures, covering a broader range of products, and reducing the flexibility of provisions in the system. In 1986, when MFA IV was negotiated, coverage was extended to additional fibers such as silk, ramie, linen, and jute.

The MFA quotas were in conflict with GATT's general preference for customs tariffs instead of measures that restrict quantities. They were also incompatible with the GATT principle of equal treatment of all trading partners, as the MFA quotas specified how much the importing country was going to accept from individual exporting countries.

The 1974 MFA did not include quotas for LDCs like Bangladesh, as it did not have any significant garment industry that posed a threat to developed countries. However, as Bangladesh became more successful in exporting garments, it faced MFA restrictions imposed by France and the UK in 1984 and the US in 1985. The immediate impacts of the MFA restrictions on Bangladesh were adverse and manifold: those led to the closure of a large number of factories and

(*continued*)

Box 3.1 (continued)
resulted in the unemployment of many workers, mostly females. Those also caused a temporary dip in bank lending and investments in the garment sector.

When the World Trade Organization (WTO) was established in 1995 at the end of the Uruguay Round of GATT, it was decided to bring the textile trade under the jurisdiction of the WTO. The Agreement on Textiles and Clothing of the WTO provided for the gradual dismantling of the quotas that existed under the MFA. This process was completed on 1 January 2005. However, large tariffs remained in place on textile products.

In the first half of 2005, exports from China to the West grew by 100 percent or more in many items. This led the US and EU to seriously consider invoking safeguards to put brakes on garment imports from China. This led to the negotiation, leading to an agreement between the EU and China, in June 2005, on a three-year "transitional arrangement" which set ceilings on annual growth of main categories of exports to about 10 percent until trade was liberalized in 2008. The US and China made a similar agreement in November 2005, which set quotas covering nearly half of China's garment imports into the US by the end of 2008. Owing to the safeguards imposed against China by the US and the European Union, the withdrawal of MFA quotas did not impede growth of the garment industry in Bangladesh.

Some of the adverse impact of MFA on the trade of developing countries was nullified by a trade concession provided by advanced countries, called the Generalized System of Preferences (GSP). At the behest of UNCTAD, the US Trade Act of 1974 introduced GSP to promote exports from developing countries. This legislation gave the president the authority to grant preferences for LDC products excluding import-sensitive goods such as textiles and apparel. As is apparent, it did not include the items that were of greatest export interest of developing countries like Bangladesh. However, Bangladesh did receive some, albeit small, benefits from the US GSP until it was excluded by President Obama in 2013 over workers' safety and labor rights violations in the country's garment industry. (Bangladesh was the only South Asian country excluded from the

(*continued*)

Box 3.1 (continued)
US GSP benefits.) Bangladesh exports to the US are now subject to very high tariffs. According to PEW Research Center, nearly all Bangladeshi imports are subject to US tariffs equivalent to 15.2 percent, which was the highest average rate among all countries in 2018 (Desilver 2018).

Bangladesh has, however, benefited significantly from the GSP of the European Union from its program of Everything But Arms (EBA), which came into force in March 2001. That allows all LDC imports to the EU duty-free and quota-free, with the exception of armaments. EU is currently the largest market for Bangladeshi exports.

whose chairman Kim Woo-Choong met with Noorul Khan and signed, on July 4, 1978, a five-year partnership agreement with Desh Garments. This agreement included collaboration on technical training, machinery and fabric purchases, plant start-ups, and marketing. Under this collaborative agreement, Desh would provide land and labor while Daewoo would bring capital, supervise the use of new machinery it sold to Desh, advise on production, procure raw materials, and market the company's products internationally. For its service, Desh would pay Daewoo royalties for technical training and supervision, equivalent to 3 percent of sales, and a sales commission for marketing services, equivalent to 5 percent of the sales, during the contract period. The agreement did not include any investment or financing on the part of Daewoo other than for fabric and other intermediate inputs purchased on short-term credit. Under the agreement, 130 Bangladeshi work supervisors were sent to the Pusan Garment Factory in Korea for intensive training for on-the-job skills and hands-on experience in running a factory. On completion of their training, these supervisors returned to Bangladesh, along with three Daewoo engineers assigned to install the machinery and start production. Three production lines were set up within five months, with 450 machines and 500 workers. An additional three production lines were set up to train new recruits (Dinh et al. 2013).

Desh made its first export in 1980, a shipment of 43,000 shirts valued at $56,000. As Desh's experience and reputation grew, it decided to terminate its collaborative agreement with Daewoo in 1981, about 18 months after factory operations began. Although formal collaboration with

Daewoo had ended, it continued to collaborate informally with Daewoo through consultation and information exchange.

The significance of Desh in the economic history of Bangladesh is far beyond that of a business entity. Desh played a catalytic role in creating and fostering the growth of an industry, virtually from scratch, an industry which went on to become the country's single-most important manufacturing as well as export business. Among Bangladeshi enterprises, it was Desh that, for the first time, made an international breakthrough in acquiring and mastering the knowledge of running an international business and spread it among the future entrepreneurs in the country.[2] The learning and technology transfer that this single project catalyzed was unprecedented; by the end of the 1980s, 115 out of the 130 Desh supervisory staff who were first trained in Daewoo factories in South Korea became entrepreneurs and set up their own firms (Dinh et al. 2013).

How does one explain the success of Desh? The business instinct of Khan was definitely important, but no less important was the political support he could harness in support of his project. According to Khan (2013), it was the then President Zia who took the initiative to link up Noorul Quader Khan with Kim Woo-Choong, the chairman of Daewoo. Moreover, the President's support also assured the South Koreans that "unexpected institutional problems with regard to the joint venture would be dealt with or at least addressed" (Khan 2013, 104). Finally, this political support—as well as his own bureaucratic connections, he being a former bureaucrat—helped to overcome the bureaucratic red tape and relatively quick adoption of a simple but ingenious institutional innovation, known as back-to-back letter of credit. This mechanism—which allowed Bangladeshi producers to use their export orders as collateral to borrow from local banks to finance raw materials imports—helped producers to economize on their working capital and foreign exchange, thereby achieving substantial economy in the cost of producing garments.

Also, quickly established was the bonded warehouse system to circumvent heavy and complex customs duties on imported inputs. In a heavily protected trade regime like that of Bangladesh, it was difficult to compete in the global market as producers had to pay several times the world price for raw materials. Daewoo was very familiar with the special bonded warehouse system in Korea and advised Khan to press for such a bonded warehouse facility that would make their raw materials more price-competitive.[3]

Impact of the RMG Industry

Over time, the RMG industry has blossomed into the most significant manufacturing industry in the country: Bangladesh is now the second largest exporter of RMGs after China. In 2017, the industry's contribution to exports exceeded $28 billion, which amounted to more than 80 percent of exports. The industry now has approximately 5000 domestic garment companies, which employ more than 4 million workers, 80 percent of whom are women (BGMEA 2018). The RMG industry, by providing employment and income, has been a game changer for a large cohort of poor, vulnerable women, mostly displaced illiterate migrants from rural areas.

Other than income and employment, recent research suggests that the RMG industry had other positive social impacts on marriage and fertility behavior. First, it changed parents' attitude toward schooling and work, thereby leading to the postponement of early marriage and childbirth (Haeth and Mobarak 2015). Second, it had a salutary impact on female empowerment, as reflected in many diverse ways: it imbued a sense of self-esteem in female garment workers who could now exercise greater freedom in choosing their husbands; it also provided female workers greater control over family income, leading to greater decision-making power within the household and a larger voice in the social sphere (Karim 2014).

To sustain its tempo of growth in the face of increasing global competition, the RMG industry will need to move up the value ladder and develop stronger backward linkages. So far, these twin desiderata of robust growth have largely eluded the industry, which continues to be dominated by low value-added RMGs whose global competitiveness relies on low wages. It may be noted that the monthly minimum wage for unskilled garment workers in Bangladesh is still rock-bottom, one of the lowest in the world: it was $68 compared with Vietnam's $85–$128 and China's $156–$266 (International Labor Organization 2014).

Major Issues in the RMG Industry

The two major issues that had been a constant source of consternation for the RMG industry are workers' safety and labor rights. Since inception, the country's garment factories have been grim sweatshops and plagued by occasional industrial accidents, the deadliest of which was the April 2013 collapse of an eight-storied building, Rana Plaza, housing five garment factories on the outskirts of Dhaka. This accident resulted in the deaths of more than 1100 people and injuries to many more hundreds. The Rana Plaza tragedy was the worst industrial accident in Bangladesh history and the deadliest in the world since the 1984 Bhopal disaster in India.

The Rana Plaza collapse brought the world's attention to worker safety and prompted two Western initiatives to improve conditions in the Bangladeshi factories with business ties with Western brands. These two 2013 initiatives—the Accord on Fire and Building Safety in Bangladesh and the Alliance for Bangladesh Worker Safety—stipulated a set of fire and building safety standards and gave factories until the summer of 2018 to improve conditions. Any factory that did not meet these standards risked losing its relationship with the Western brands that were party to Accord and Alliance. However, since then, notable safety improvements have taken place in Bangladesh garment factories, thanks to the cooperation and financial support from Accord and Alliance as well as from the International Finance Corporation (IFC).[4]

Unfortunately, no such commensurate improvement has so far taken place in the area of workers' rights—in particular, freedom of association and the right to collective bargaining, as well as responsible business conduct. Workers' rights have been succinctly summarized by Applebaum and Lichtenstein:

> Key protections in labor law, from pregnancy leave to limits on overtime hours, are routinely ignored. Verbal abuse of workers is standard operating procedure, and physical and sexual abuse is not uncommon. Any attempt by workers to address these issues by advocating for better conditions and wages is met with swift and harsh repression. Until the government came under significant pressure in 2013, there were no unions in Bangladesh, and in the face of continued resistance from factory management, less than 3 percent of workers are currently organized. The "trouble-makers" are fired, often threatened with police repression and, increasingly, face violent retaliation. If there is a race to the bottom, Bangladesh has won it. (Applebaum and Lichtenstein 2016, 25)

The government enacted a labor-law amendment in 2013, but this amendment did not contribute much to improving workers' conditions. Harassment of workers still persists unabated while there has been little increase in workers' wages or benefits since 2013. Only recently did the government decide to fix the minimum wage (inclusive of all benefits) at Tk 8000 (which is around $90), a rate widely rejected by the workers' representatives (*The Daily Star* 2018).

Many of the issues in the RMG industry reflect the failure of the government in its role as a regulator. The government has delegated most of its regulatory role to the Bangladesh Garment Manufacturers and Exporters Association (BGMEA), a trade facilitation body for the industry. Members of the government—which include a large number of members of the parliament—have significant financial interests in this sector. Consequently, there is a very clear financial incentive for the government to give the industry as much of a free pass as possible.

At the early stage of development of the industry, when the government had limited bureaucratic capacity to handle the complexities of global trade, it delegated to BGMEA the authority to manage the quota system, regulate certain transactions, and collect certain fees. With time, BGMEA's authority has not diminished but only grown. It now enjoys a near stranglehold on exports: only factories that hold BGMEA membership are allowed to export woven garments, with some exceptions. The group also regulates the import of fabric and issues certificates of origin. It has arbitration committees to settle disputes and administers the often-complex practice of subcontracting (Yardley 2013).

In the past, BGMEA had acted in the dual capacity of a regulator and a facilitator of the business. However, such delegation has become counterproductive in some sense; the government needs to gradually disentangle the twin role played by BGMEA. It has been claimed that BGMEA had an unfair influence in diluting the 2013 labor-law amendment to protect workers' rights, an act which might have been a short-term win, but represents a long-term folly for BGMEA. It must be recognized that the continued long-term growth of the industry must be anchored in a congenial work environment that balances business profitability with workers' rights, which includes protection from arbitrary arrests and prosecution, and workers' wage compensation, which covers basic food, education, medicine, and housing.

International Migration and Remittances

The second driver of the Bangladesh economy is international labor migration and remittances. Although Bangladesh has a long history of international migration, it experienced a spectacular rise in international migration to the Middle East in the 1970s following the first oil shock. In the wake of the Yum Kippur war in 1973, oil price quadrupled and the Middle Eastern oil-producing countries became affluent overnight. The second oil shock came following the 1979 Iranian Revolution when there was a further spike in the oil price. The immediate consequence was an enormous increase in the incomes of the Middle Eastern oil-producing economies. For example, per capita income in Saudi Arabia jumped from less than $1000 in 1970 to more than $6000 in 1975, which went up further to more than $16,000 in 1980. In the mid-1970s, with this new-found wealth, these countries undertook ambitious physical infrastructure development programs, with expenditures running into billions of dollars. However, these countries suffered from a shortage of both the workers and the technical skills required to implement such programs. This infrastructure boom in the Middle East created unprecedented economic opportunities for workers from Bangladesh as well as other Asian labor-surplus economies. In Bangladesh, this process received an extra fillip as the government adopted labor migration as a part of an overall development strategy in 1976. The economic imperative behind the strategy was twofold: The export of labor would ameliorate the acute unemployment and underemployment facing the economy and the resulting remittances would be a major source of foreign exchange for the economy as well as enhance income of the remittance-receiving families.

Labor Migration: When, Where, and Who

What began as a trickle, an outflow of a few thousand workers to the Middle East in 1976, became an avalanche by the 1990s, running into hundreds of thousands of workers. From 1976 to 2017, the total outflow of workers has exceeded 11 million (BMET 2018). As there are no data on return-migrants, it is difficult to estimate precisely the net outflow of migrants as well as the net stock. According to the United Nations Population Division estimate, in 2017, there were about 7.5 million international migrants from Bangladesh, representing about 4.5 percent of the country's population or more than 11 percent of its labor force (United Nations 2017).

The three countries that host more than 80 percent of Bangladeshi migrant workers are Saudi Arabia (around 30 percent), the United Arab Emirates (UAE) (around 20 percent), and Oman (around 12 percent). (The numbers within parentheses denote the percentage of total Bangladeshi migrant workers hosted by the country [BMET 2018].) The migration process to these countries has followed a virtual stop-and-go cycle. Among these countries, Saudi Arabia stopped issuing visas in 2008, which was later resumed in 2017, mainly to females as domestic help, a category that is exempted from its Nitaqat program—the Saudization program. Bangladesh's entry into this job category was also facilitated by the fact that the Philippines, Indonesia, and Sri Lanka, the three major sources of female workers, stopped deploying female workers since 2015, alleging ill-treatment in Saudi Arabia.

The UAE imposed a visa ban on Bangladeshi workers in 2012 which was recently lifted in 2018 after a six-year hiatus. Oman had an embargo on hiring all categories of workers, from 1995 to 2007, when it decided to lift its ban on unskilled workers. In January 2018, Oman again imposed a six-month visa ban on all foreign workers, including those from Bangladesh, across 87 sectors.

Other important destinations in the Middle East include Kuwait, Qatar, Bahrain, Lebanon, Jordan, and Libya. Of these, the relatively new ones are Lebanon and Jordan, which became active since the beginning of the 2000s, while Libya became largely dormant due to the outbreak of the civil war in 2014. Kuwait had an off-again and on-again ban on Bangladeshi workers: it imposed a ban in 2007 to lift it again in 2014 with the exception of domestic male help.

In South East Asia, the major destinations are Malaysia and Singapore, which respectively host about 8 percent and 6 percent of Bangladeshi migrants. In 1994, Malaysia opened its door to Bangladeshi workers, but the door was shut again in 1997. The ban continued for 10 years till 2007, only to be reimposed in 2009. In 2016, Malaysia signed a bilateral agreement with Bangladesh to resume import of workers from Bangladesh. As Malaysia and Singapore are popular destinations among potential migrants, many workers move to those countries through irregular channels as illegals.

In Europe, Italy, which hosts only 1 percent of total migrants, is a major and growing destination, and provides an alternative to the brutal working conditions and pervasive workers' rights violations that are commonplace in Gulf countries. However, most recent migrants in Italy arrived irregularly via Libya, seeking asylum rather than work.[5]

As expected, the migrants from Bangladesh are mostly young: about two-thirds of workers who migrated between 1990 and 2017 belonged to the age bracket of 15–34 years (United Nations 2017). The workers who migrate overseas are mostly males. Partly, this preponderance of males is due to the fact that Bangladesh had often pursued restrictive policies toward female migration, ranging from total ban to various types of partial restrictions with respect to age and occupation. However, since the beginning of this century, the government has adopted a more liberal policy, leading to a gradual rise in the population of female migrants. The current stock of female migrants is estimated at more than 750,000—of which the UAE hosts about 27 percent, Saudi Arabia about 16 percent, Lebanon about 31 percent, and Jordan 9 percent. In most countries, the vast majority of female workers are employed as domestic help; however, in the latter two countries, there are female migrants who are employed in garment factories.

The skill composition of migrant workers is heavily skewed toward unskilled and semi-skilled. According to BMET (cited in International Labor Organization 2015), of all those who migrated between 1976 and 2012,), a mere 2 percent were professionals (such as doctors, engineers, teachers, and nurses) and less than one third of the workers were skilled (such as garment workers, drivers, computer operators, and electricians). And the vast majority, about two-thirds of the Bangladeshi workers are unskilled (such as domestic workers, agricultural workers, and hotel workers) and semi-skilled (such as tailors and masons) (International Labor Organization 2015). In other words, the outflow of workers from Bangladesh was not a brain drain—an exodus of brains—but more of a brawn drain, a massive departure of young, able-bodied, less skilled men and women in quest of overseas work.

Despite claims to the contrary, this dominance of unskilled workers in international migration did not dampen the flow of remittances, rather it might have had some positive impact. While professionals/skilled migrants typically earn more, it is presumed that they will remit more, a contention which is not necessarily true. The fact is that these "elite" migrants often leave home lock, stock, and barrel; and even when they do not leave permanently, they are more likely to spend greater time abroad and reunite with their immediate family outside the home country. In either instance, professional/skilled workers have less incentive to remit their income home than unskilled workers. This intuition is corroborated by a recent body of international evidence which suggests that the brain drain is associated with a smaller propensity to remit (Faini January 2007); or that remittances tend to decrease as the share of migrants with tertiary education increases (Niimi et al. 2010). These findings have obvious ramifications for international migration policy of labor-exporting countries.

Remittances: Size and Impact

As the flow of international migration increased over time, so did the volume of remittances. Starting with a modest amount of remittances of $23 million in 1976, the flow of remittances reached $13.5 billion in 2017.

The Gulf countries are the most important source for remittance, with Saudi Arabia, and the UAE leading the pack, both accounting for more than $2 billion in 2017. In East Asia, Malaysia accounted for more than $1 billion in 2017 (BMET 2018).

Ranked as one of the top ten remittance-receiving countries of the world, Bangladesh now receives more remittances than either foreign aid or FDI; indeed, in 2017, remittances exceeded three times the inflows of foreign aid and FDI combined.

As is obvious, remittances have become increasingly important as a source of development finance. It has significantly relaxed the foreign exchange constraint as well as the savings constraint of the country. As a percentage of GDP, remittances have reached more than 10 percent in 2012; then, the rate, however, declined gradually to around 5 percent in 2017. In other words, remittances have added 5–10 percentage points to the national savings rate, which had a salutary impact on the growth trajectory of the economy. Although the economics literature speaks about the possible adverse impact of remittances on the real exchange rate and export competitiveness, there is no evidence to suggest that such adverse effects exist in the case of Bangladesh.

There is a good deal of international evidence on the positive impact of remittances on poverty. A cross-country study, using data from 71 countries, reported that a 10 percent increase in per capita remittances led, on average, to a 3.5 percent decline in poverty (Adams and Page 2005). A similar study by Asian Development Bank Institute, using panel data from 1981 to 2014 for ten Asian developing countries, including Bangladesh, reported that a 1 percent increase in international remittances as a percentage of GDP led to a 22.6 percent decline in the poverty gap ratio and a 16.0 percent decline in the poverty severity ratio (Yoshino et al. 2017). More direct, but suggestive, evidence on Bangladesh came from the Household Income & Expenditure Survey (HIES) 2010. It indicated that remittances had a significant impact on household consumption and savings—income, consumption, and savings per month were all higher for the remittance-receiving households compared with those without (by an average 82 percent, 38 percent, and 107 percent respectively). In 2010, about 13 percent of the remittance-receiving households were below the poverty line, compared with about 34 percent of non-receiving households, when the poverty incidence rate was about 32 percent nationally (World Bank 2012).

The nexus between international migration and poverty reduction was further corroborated by a longitudinal study by the Refugee Migration Movement Research Unit (RMMRU). According to this study, cited by Hussain (2014), only 13 percent of the migrant households were below the poverty line, compared with 40 percent of the nonmigrant households. The survey covered particularly those groups that were either below poverty line or that experienced occasional deficits, or "break-even" situations at the time of their first international migration. When migrants were compared with nonmigrants in terms of living standards, it was found that migrants enjoyed a better living standard compared to nonmigrants in terms of their quality of housing, access to electricity, and sanitary toilets. While the study found little difference between migrant and nonmigrant households in schooling of their children, international migrants spent more on private tutoring compared to nonmigrants. This differential existed also in terms of family health expenditures: migrants spent more on health services compared to nonmigrants. Compared to nonmigrants, migrant households spent significantly more on food and other related expenditures, which are important for a poor economy that has nutritional issues. Finally, a higher percentage of migrants invested in new homesteads compared with nonmigrants; moreover, in home construction, migrant households spent a hefty 75 percent more than nonmigrants (Hussain 2014).

The positive impact of remittances on expenditure on human capital formation has been confirmed by other studies as well. A BBS study on the use of remittances indicates that food, purchase of land and loan repayment were the three most important items followed by expenditures on education and health (BBS 2014). It is often suggested that such items as food consumption and land acquisition do not contribute toward human capital formation. This is a fallacious argument because in a poor society where nutrition and adequacy of food are serious concerns, food consumption is as much an investment in human capital as any other item. Similarly, improvements in rural housing, much of which were due to migrants, contributed to rural sanitation—including the success in eliminating open defecation. Another survey by the International Migration Organization (IOM), cited by World Bank, reported a different allocation of expenditure—more toward education and health and less toward purchase of land and construction of houses (World Bank 2012). Whatever be the allocation made by migrants, they were rational and served Bangladesh well.

Migration and Remittances: Major Issues

Despite the salience of international labor migration and inward remittances in initiating and sustaining development in Bangladesh, the process has been fraught with myriad issues. The first major issue relates to the costs for Bangladeshi workers, which are among the highest in the world. In the absence of direct hiring by employers, almost all the recruitments in the Gulf countries involve a labyrinthine recruitment network, encompassing the international sponsoring companies to intermediaries in the host country to the recruiting agencies in the home country[6] and their subagents, known as dalals—and the cumbersome *kafala* visa process—where the migrant visas are bought and sold to the highest bidders. The whole process is highly exploitative and almost predatory.

A survey of recently deployed migrant workers by Refugee and Migratory Movements Research Unit of University of Dhaka (RMMRU) found that the average migration cost currently stands at $4800. The World Bank initiative Knowledge Network on Migration and Development (KNOMAD) reported in 2014 that Bangladeshis had to work for nine months in Kuwait simply to recoup the money that they had spent to finance migration. This contrasts sharply with the situation in other countries. To recover the migration expenses, Indian workers had to work for two and a half months while Sri Lankans for only 1 month. For other countries, it takes, on average, workers 17 months to recoup their recruiter fees and travel costs to Saudi Arabia, around 11 months for the UAE and Oman, and roughly ten months for Bahrain, Libya, and Qatar (Abrar 2017).

In addition to excessive financial costs of migration, potential Bangladeshi migrants are often victims of smuggling or trafficking. There are many reasons for this, one being the complexity of the recruitment networks that makes it difficult to track down such crimes and prosecute the traffickers successfully. In the past, the conviction rates for trafficking had been extremely low for various reasons—including the fact that most laws in this area were recent, and the national criminal justice system did not have adequate expertise as well as resources to successfully handle such prosecutions.

The second concern relates to violation of migrants' rights. Belonging to the most vulnerable segment in the host countries, migrants often suffer serious violations of their human rights, including abusive or exploitative working conditions and ill-treatment by immigration or law enforcement authorities. In most countries, migrant workers are deprived of basic workplace rights and protections; they are afforded limited access to social security, if any; finally, they are subject to systemic discrimination and widespread xenophobia and prejudice. Female migrants, who work mostly as domestic workers, face even more abuses inside employers' homes.

The adverse work conditions, in conjunction with excessive workload, poor living conditions, and mental stress, have taken a heavy toll on the otherwise young Bangladeshi migrant workforce. From 2005 to November 2017, more than 33,000 migrant workers returned home dead in body bags. In the first 11 months of 2017, Bangladesh airports received more than 3000 dead bodies, at an average rate of 8 to 10 daily (*Dhaka Tribune* 2017). (However, not all of these deaths are work-related.) Similarly, newspapers are abuzz with reports of hordes of female domestic workers, returning home, after being physically abused and financially defrauded.

Bangladesh has adopted a wide array of policies to protect its expatriate workers. In 1982, Bangladesh enacted the Emigration Ordinance to regulate and monitor the departure of migrant workers. In 1998, Bangladesh signed the UN's International Convention on the "Protection of Rights of All Migrant Workers and Members of Their Families", which is one of the migrant-sending countries' most important political tools in negotiations with countries that rely on foreign labor. In 2006, the Overseas Employment Policy was formulated to provide workers the rights to choose quality employment. In 2013, Bangladesh legislated the Overseas Employment and Migrants Act, which repeals the Emigration Ordinance 1982 and makes its provisions consistent with the international treaties and conventions signed by the country. The Act is an overall framework to govern migration by protecting migrant rights. It includes provisions to facilitate return of migrants during emergencies, clamp down on fraudulent practices, and hold recruitment agencies accountable. Despite this plethora of ordinances and policies, the plight of Bangladeshi migrants remains highly vulnerable and has improved little over the years.

Finally, in recent years, remittances have exhibited wide fluctuations. Although the out-migration of workers has been on the rise, remittances, after two years of decline, hovered around $15 billion in 2018—the level of 1915. One explanation that has been advanced relates to the increasing dominance of lower-paying female domestic helpers. The other explanation relates to *hundi*, an informal money-transfer system, which is cheaper, faster, and has increasingly become more efficient with digital apps. The exchange rate offered by *hundi* is also more attractive than the official rate. All these may have made *hundi* more attractive to many workers to transfer their savings. It is suggested that *hundi* is the conduit of choice for capital flight from Bangladesh—which exceeded $61 billion between 2005 and 2014, according to Global Financial Integrity, an American research and advocacy group—and the mechanism is under-invoicing of imports, which are being paid for by migrant workers savings, thereby shrinking official remittances (*Economist* 2017).

Agriculture

The third driver of development for Bangladesh is agriculture. A marker of success for agriculture is the breakthrough in food production, which helped to transform the economy from a state of being chronically food-deficit to one of food adequacy. This represents a major achievement for a country faced with enormous constraints of rising population, shrinking cultivable land, and an adverse natural environment.

Advances in Food Production

In the wake of independence, hunger and destitution were pervasive, a state that reached a nadir in 1974, when the economy was engulfed by one of the worst famines in human history, resulting in 1.5 million deaths. This trauma of poignant poverty, vulnerability, and suffering was etched on people's collective memory, which led to a national sense of priority to assure food security.

The major food items produced by Bangladesh are rice, wheat, potato, pulses, oilseeds, sugarcane, and vegetables, of which rice and wheat are the most important, accounting for more than four-fifths of the cropped land. This inordinate emphasis on cereal production, especially rice, stems from the fact that people derive a large percentage of their calorie intake from cereals. While rice is produced all over the country, the production of wheat is limited only to the northwestern part of the country for climatic reasons. Of the other food items, production in pulses, oilseeds, and sugarcane has, in recent years, experienced a decline, which has been compensated by some increase in the production of vegetables and potatoes.

Bangladesh has made remarkable progress over the past four-plus decades toward food security; for example, rice production increased by three and half times between 1972 and 2014, from 9.8 to 34.4 million tons. Since 1995, Bangladesh experienced one of the fastest rates of productivity growth in the world, averaging 2.7 percent per year, which was second only to China. In the 1980s, growth in rice production kept pace with population growth; however, in the 1990s, there was a further acceleration in the growth of rice production, a rate that outstripped population growth by a significant margin.

Factors Behind Success

There are several factors behind this rapid transformation, which include an early and sustained investment in agricultural research; increased outlays in rural infrastructure—irrigation and roads; improved access to credit; and the deregulation of product and inputs markets. All these factors helped to create an incentive framework for productivity growth.

Agricultural research was key to the transformation process. The National Agricultural Research Systems, in partnership with international agricultural research organizations such as International Rice Research Institute (IRRI) and the International Maize and Wheat Improvement Center (CIMMYT), had released over the years a large number of modern varieties of crops including rice varieties. This process started in the 1970s when new varieties of seeds started to come on stream. Over time, as these improved, modern varieties began replacing low-yielding traditional varieties, there was a surge in yield, reduction in per unit cost of production, as well as an increase in profitability. Consequently, there was a decline in the real price of agricultural products over time without ever jeopardizing production incentives for the farmers. Public investments in agriculture and liberalization of input and output markets helped to further bolster the incentive structure.

Since the 1970s, the government, with the assistance of international development agencies, has made significant investments in irrigation, flood control and drainage, riverbank erosion mitigation, and rural infrastructure. Rural infrastructure in the form of rural roads and rural electricity has had a significant impact on agricultural productivity. Improved rural roads facilitated easier movement of produce from the farm to the market and led to a reduction in the cost of food transportation and an increase in freight traffic. Flood control, drainage, and riverbank erosion mitigation helped protect and expand farmland. Rural electrification was also significant in facilitating electrification of irrigation pumps and increasing agricultural productivity. Finally, agricultural credit has been a priority for successive governments. Credit disbursements from public and private commercial banks had been on the increase in recent years. Bangladesh Bank has encouraged commercial banks to expand farm loans—it is mandatory for all banks to deliver agricultural loans at a subsidized interest rate. In terms of institutions, infrastructure, and policy, the economy has undergone significant transformation over time since independence.

At Independence in 1971, Bangladesh adopted socialism as a state principle and pursued a public sector–led development strategy in all sectors of the economy. In agriculture, a public-sector corporation, Bangladesh Agricultural Development Corporation (BADC), was accorded virtual monopoly over the procurement and distribution of subsidized agricultural inputs such as seed, fertilizer, irrigation equipment, and so on. However, the system proved to be highly inefficient and was replaced, in the 1980s, through a series of market-oriented reforms. These reforms led to a gradual reduction of subsidies and allowed the private sector a greater role in procuring and distributing inputs and importing food grains. However, all this did not always lead to the intended consequences, thereby requiring further adjustments in the system (Jaim and Akter 2012).

An important outcome of this market liberalization and privatization policy has been the withdrawal of import restrictions on pumps and small diesel engines, reductions in import duties, and a marked reduction in prices of irrigation equipment. Consequently, irrigation equipment has become more widely available and affordable to the farmers, leading to a large outpouring of private investments in minor irrigation equipment—that is, low-lift pumps and shallow tube wells. This increase in minor irrigation equipment led to a rapid expansion in irrigated area. This process was further facilitated by the emergence of a water market that permitted small and marginal farmers, who could not afford to invest in irrigation equipment, access to irrigation services. This wide availability of low-lift pumps and shallow tube wells, in conjunction with fertilizers, helped to expand rice production in the previously negligible dry season (the Boro crop).[7] Since the late1990s, the Boro crop had emerged as the major contributor to the country's rice output, surpassing the Aman crop, representing a structural shift in rice production—from a largely weather-dependent crop to an irrigated crop, which is more sensitive to the quality of government policy than to the vagaries of nature (Deb 2016).

Beginning in the 1980s, a similar set of market-oriented reforms was introduced in the fertilizer market, relating to the privatization of sale, distribution, and import of fertilizers. However, these reforms led to some unintended consequences in the fertilizer market—such as frequent price hikes, unbalanced use of fertilizer, lack of timeliness in delivery, and fertilizer adulteration. In response to these problems, government made a course correction in the 1990s that entailed taking over the wholesale distribution from the private sector, reintroducing fertilizer subsidy, and operating a buffer stock to stabilize fertilizer prices. As these actions did not fully address the problems, the government reverted to a more open system, but with a tighter control of the process. This calibration of the system led to significant improvement in the availability of fertilizers, but the price of fertilizers, despite the government subsidies, remained relatively high.

In 1993, the government introduced a comprehensive seed policy which significantly liberalized the market. Even though the policy delegated the prime role of seed production and marketing to the government agencies, it allowed the private sector and NGOs into seed production and marketing. Since the introduction of the policy, supply of quality seeds has been on the increase. The private sector was mainly focused on the supply and production of hybrid seeds that yielded a higher return on investments. With import restrictions relaxed, there was also some entry of multinational companies into import business. With the liberalization of the seed trade, there has been an increase in the availability of quality seed, although price remains an issue (Jaim and Akter 2012).

Historically, food imports were partly met by food aid, which supplied two-thirds of total wheat imports (about 1 million tons per year) and less than 1 percent of rice imports, and partly by the government through its commercial imports. A major landmark reform in this regard was the liberalization of private-sector food imports since the early 1990s, a reform which helped to stabilize the supply as well as the price in times of natural disaster. The growth in private rice marketing as well as privately held rice stocks made it possible for the government to reduce its own food grain stocks and streamline procurement, with the welcome consequence that it helped the government to reduce its budget on food subsidies considerably.

Despite Bangladesh's success in augmenting food availability, the poor and vulnerable still suffer from the problems of inadequate food intakes and chronic malnutrition. The current safety-net program in Bangladesh is largely food-based and tied to the Public Food Distribution System (PFDS). The government provides emergency relief during periods of natural disasters, through targeted food distributions, and helps stabilize the market price of food, especially rice. Other food-distribution programs have explicit development objectives—such as development of rural infrastructure, boosting school enrollment, and so on. To achieve those ends, the government maintains food stocks, procures rice and wheat from farmers, and, when necessary, imports food either commercially or as food aid.

At independence from Britain in 1947, all countries in the Indian subcontinent inherited a set of laws, institutions, and practices that provided tight government control of food grain production, supply, and distribution. These systems for food grain control have evolved differently across the countries in the subcontinent. Bangladesh has adopted a liberal, market-oriented approach to food and agricultural policy reforms: it has liberalized its domestic as well as international food grain trade, by reducing public presence in food grain procurement and distribution, allowing licensed private traders to import food grain, and dismantling prior restrictions on private stockholding and marketing, and withdrawing urban and rural consumer ration subsidies in favor of targeted, in-kind, often "for work" programs. It is said that, unlike many other countries, Bangladesh has implemented its pro-market food policy reforms without triggering violence or food riots (Ahmed and Haggleblade 2000).

Many Shades of Success

What does the data suggest about the goal of self-sufficiency of food, a stated objective of the government? One way to look at it is to compare the domestic supply of food against the aggregate food requirement of the country. This comparison would suggest that Bangladesh is on the brink of food self-sufficiency, producing more than the minimum requirement in normal years while slipping below the threshold in years of natural disasters—drought and floods (see Table 3.1).

The final column in Table 3.1 indicates the food surplus or deficit the country is experiencing. The column shows the country has had a surplus in recent years, although it is not clear how net food requirements were calculated and what assumptions went into constructing the table, especially since rice is regularly imported.

The second way to interpret self-sufficiency is to examine the volume of net import of food. In this respect, despite the rise in the domestic food production, the target of attaining self-sufficiency of food—meaning zero net import—has proved elusive. Recent data suggest that imports of cereals have also shot up markedly. During the period 2013–2017, the average import of cereal was 5.2 million tons, which increased to 8.8 million tons in 2017 and will remain high at 8.3 million tons in 2018. Though food import has increased over time, some of which was not necessarily

Table 3.1 Food surplus/deficit in Bangladesh—1996/97–2016/17

Year/ Items	*Midyear population (in millions)*	*Net food grain requirement*	*Gross food grain production*	*Net food grain production*	*Food grain surplus*
1996/97	123	20,364	20,336	18,302.4	−2062
1997/98	125	20,695.5	20,665	18,598.5	−2097
1998/99	127	21,026.63	21,813	19,631.7	−1395
2001/02	133	22,020.01	25,905	23,314.5	1294
2003/04	137.54	24,548.83	27,442	24,697.8	149
2004/05	139.78	24,948.63	26,133	23,519.7	−1429
2005/06	141.8	25,309.17	27,266	24,538.5	−771
2006/07	142.6	25,685.78	28,055	24,666.29	−1019
2007/08	144.6	26,046.32	29,775	26,176.68	130
2008/09	146.5	26,390.79	32,166	28,280.61	1890
2009/10	148.4	26,717.42	33,158	29,210	2492
2010/11	150.4	27,058.33	34,513	30,342.28	3284
2011/12	152.3	28,295.06	34,869	30,655.32	2360
2012/13	154.1	28,629	35,088	30,839.79	2210
2013/14	156	28,982	35,657	31,339.13	2357
2014/15	158	29,354	36,058	31,690.6	2337
2015/16	160	29,726	36,058	31,691	1965
2016/17	162	30,097	35,115	30,862	765

Source: BBS and Ministry of Food and Disaster Management (http://fpmu.gov.bd/fpmu-database/0103.htm)

Note: Quantities are expressed in thousand metric tons

warranted by food shortage, but due to increase in demand of affluent urban consumers for finer varieties. Both the government and private sectors were engaged in cereal import, but the bulk of the recent import was done by the private sector.

The concept of food self-sufficiency has been the subject of a good deal of controversy in recent years. Critics note that most attempts to become fully self-sufficient can be expensive; they can create market uncertainties, exacerbate domestic price instability, and discard benefits from the principle of comparative advantage. This has led the *Economist* to argue that food self-sufficiency is not just a bad idea; it is a potentially lethal one and should be discarded (*Economist* 2013).

The idea which has in recent years acquired greater currency is the concept of food security, which is defined as the condition in which all people, at all times, have physical, social, and economic access to sufficient safe and nutritious food that meets their dietary needs and food preferences for an active and healthy life. This concept has three dimensions: (i) adequacy of food supply through increased domestic production and imports; (ii) access to food through public distribution and expanded safety net programs; and (iii) increased food utilization and nutrition.

Recent years have witnessed a good deal of progress in food availability, as measured in terms of per capita caloric availability. According to the Food and Agriculture Organization (FAO), per capita food supplies have increased from 2309 kcal per day equivalent in 2000 to 2435 kcal in 2004 and 2481 kcal in 2009 (FAO 2014), which is higher than several South Asian countries including India, Pakistan, Nepal, and Sri Lanka (USAID 2015). However, the average can mask the wide disparity that might exist between different income groups. This increase food availability has been accompanied by people's affordability, including that of the poor, as reflected in the decline in poverty and rising real wages (as described in the preceding chapter).

In recent years, Bangladesh has also made significant progress in food utilization, as reflected in various nutritional outcomes such as the rate of child undernutrition, the rate of stunting among children under five, and the state of maternal undernutrition. Some possible factors behind this improvement, as some quantitative studies suggest, include growth of income and wealth, education (especially maternal education), expansion of health-care coverage, and improved sanitation (Osmani et al. 2016). However, this result should be treated only as suggestive, not comprehensive, as these factors explain only about half of the variation, leaving "a measure of ignorance".

Nongovernmental Organizations

As widely acknowledged, an important driver of development in Bangladesh is NGOs, which helped to create a structure of a safety net for a large segment of the poor population and contributed in important ways toward improving health and social indicators of the populace. Following the World Bank, NGOs are defined here to mean "private organizations characterized primarily by humanitarian or cooperative, rather than commercial, objectives that pursue activities to relieve suffering, promote the interests of the poor, protect the environment, provide basic social services, or undertake community development" in developing countries (World Bank 1995, 13).

Although Bangladesh has a history of philanthropy and community engagement, the NGO, in its modern form, emerged immediately after the independence in response to the economic exigencies of the war of liberation and the massive famine of 1974 that trailed it. The two most well-known NGOs of Bangladesh—BRAC[8] and Grameen Bank—grew out of this tumultuous period.

In 1972, Fazle Hasan Abed, an expatriate Bangladeshi working in London, left his well-paying corporate job to start BRAC as a modest relief and rehabilitation effort in a remote northeastern district of Bangladesh. Shortly afterward, realizing that relief was not enough to make a sustainable improvement in poor people's lives, BRAC began experimenting with various development projects on health, education, and microfinance. BRAC—which now provides a whole gamut of services, encompassing microloans, self-employment opportunities, health services, education, and legal and human rights services—is rated as the largest NGO in the world, employing more than 100,000 people (roughly 70 percent of whom are women), reaching more than 110 million people with its services (BRAC 2017).

During the 1974 famine, Mohammed Yunus was an economics professor at Chittagong University. Greatly disillusioned with the disjunction between the abstract economic theory he was teaching and the abject poverty that surrounded the campus, he wanted to make a difference at the grassroots level. This prompted him to extend a loan of $27 to a small neighboring village community of basket-weavers who were stricken by the famine. Grameen Bank, which Yunus started as a university project with this initial loan to 42 women, has now 8.93 million borrowers (97 percent of whom are women) and more than 2500 branches. Grameen provides services in 81,400 villages, covering more than 97 percent of the total villages in Bangladesh (Grameen Bank 2018). In recognition of its achievements, Grameen Bank was awarded the 2006 Nobel Peace Prize (divided into two equal parts, to Muhammad Yunus and Grameen Bank) "for their efforts to create economic and social development from below".

Since independence, Bangladesh has seen a proliferation of growth in the NGO sector. The country has 2619 registered NGOs, of which the vast majority, 2370, are local NGOs (NGO Affairs Bureau 2018). There are many reasons for this dramatic growth of NGOs[9]: First and foremost, the death and devastation that followed in the immediate postindependence period jolted many altruistic professionals—who were skeptical of the government's abilities or intentions—into action, who decided to organize their own NGOs to address the pressing social issues. Second, recent decades have seen an increasing flow of foreign aid to NGOs; as a matter of fact, many bilateral donors, such as the United States Agency for

International Development (USAID) and the Department for International Development (DFID), currently deliver a sizable proportion of their development assistance directly through NGOs. This trend is driven by a wide perception shared in the international development community that governmental agencies in most developing countries are weak; this has even led many multilateral donors to earmark some of their development assistance for on-lending or delivering by NGOs. Third, in Bangladesh, the costs of organizing and expanding NGO services have decreased over time with increasing population density, improved transportation infrastructure, and declining communication costs.

The range of activities undertaken by the NGOs in Bangladesh is dominated by microcredit. According to a World Bank survey, about 90 percent of all NGO branch offices provide credit services, followed by health (56 percent), sanitation (52 percent), and education (45 percent). Health and sanitation services include preventative cure and simple curative cure for women and children. Aside from these services, NGOs also provide other services in partnership with the central government or local government, including safety net programs, agricultural extension, social forestry, disaster management, skills training, and so on. The services provided by the NGOs are in accord with the service priorities identified by communities closely. Public awareness and advocacy are also a common area of NGO work: 93 percent of NGO branches reported awareness-raising activities, usually relating to sanitation, health, and social issues. Advocacy activities focus on issues such as violence against women, dowry land rights, access to justice, housing, and education (World Bank 2006).

Regarding financing, the NGO sector had been the recipient of a generous share of foreign assistance (see Table 3.2). The share of NGOs now constitutes about half of total development assistance received by the country. However, this does not include the development assistance received by government agencies—such as Palli Karma-Sahayak Foundation (PKSF)—and then contracted out to NGOs for on-lending or service delivery. According to a World Bank estimate, foreign aid constitutes 34 percent of total NGO expenditures. However, if microfinance programs are excluded, then foreign aid constitutes as much as 88 percent on non-microfinance programs. For microfinance NGOs, the main source of internal income is interest income, derived from lending activities. Private charity does not figure much in the financing of Bangladesh NGOs (World Bank 2006).

Table 3.2 Foreign aid flows to Bangladesh and NGO share—2000/2001–2013/14

Year	*Govt grant*	*Govt loan*	*Govt total*	*NGO grant*	*Bangladesh aid*	*NGO share in total aid*
2001–02	478.8	963.4	1442.2	208.28	687.08	30.3
2002–03	510.1	1074.9	1585	279.64	789.74	35.4
2003–04	338.5	695	1033.4	313.07	651.57	48
2004–05	244.2	1244.2	1488.4	274.02	518.22	52.9
2005–06	500.5	1067.1	1567.6	347.53	848.03	41
2006–07	590.2	1040.4	1630.6	322.61	912.81	35.3
2007–08	658.1	1403.4	2061.5	523.11	1181.21	44.3
2008–09	657.8	1189.5	1847.3	486.19	1143.99	42.5
2009–10	639.2	1588.6	2227.8	516.03	1155.23	44.7
2010–11	745.1	1031.6	1776.7	658.94	1404.04	46.9
2011–12	588	1538.5	2126.5	579.64	1167.64	49.6
2012–13	726.3	2084.7	2811	677.51	1403.81	48.3
2013–14	680.73	2403.66	3084.39	719.01	1399.74	51.37

Source: ERD, Ministry of Finance, cited by Bangladesh Financial Intelligent Unit (2015)

NB: Aid figures are in million US dollars. Shares in the last column are expressed in percentage

NGOs and Development

In Bangladesh, although microfinance is the flagship activity of NGOs, the subject of their economic and social impact has been mired in controversy. There are wildly divergent views on this matter. There are those who argue that microcredit had a significant impact on poverty in the country while there are others who argue that microcredit had little or no positive effect. Both views seem to find some corroboration in case studies. There are many cases of success with credit, where borrowers took out additional loans and continued to do so year after year, built flourishing small businesses, educated children, and improved nutrition. There are other cases that suggest that microcredit did not at all increase households' income and, in some cases, even led to a debt trap.

Econometric studies are equally ambiguous. Some studies that have found a positive impact of microcredit on poverty include Pitt and Khandker (1998), while others did not discern any such effect, for example, Roodman and Morduch (2014). This literature—which is marked by snipping and counter-snipping by authors regarding the soundness of methodology or adequacy of data—has turned the matter into an obtuse insider debate and has yielded little clarity.

Recent years have also seen the introduction of randomized control trials (RCTs) into the foray. The findings, which relate to a set of RCT studies over a number of countries other than Bangladesh, were summarized by Banerjee, Karlan, and Zinmand 2015, who discerned little evidence of the "transformative" effects of microcredit on poverty. However, given the diversity of the contexts, design of studies, and the quality of underlying data, one does not know how to generalize them—that is, their external validity—or how relevant they are for Bangladesh.

Another question that has figured with respect to microcredit is whether credit leads to female empowerment. Here, anthropological studies have reached opposite results. One such study, for example, concludes that microcredit has resulted in a new state of domination against poor women (Karim 2008) while another study opines that Grameen Bank, on average, empowers female borrowers (Hashemi et al. 1996). The latter positive view found confirmation in an econometric study that argued that microcredit programs, in providing women greater access to financial and economic resources as well as to social networks, resulted in a larger role for women in household decision making, afforded a greater bargaining power vis-à-vis their husbands, and more freedom of mobility (Pitt et al. 2006).

In the highly contentious area of microcredit, there are few agreements. However, one area where such a rare agreement exists is the role that microcredit plays in smoothing income and consumption. In rural areas, poor households face many types of economic contingencies including adverse health shocks. Here, microcredit can not only help to smooth seasonal consumption but also avert the distress sale of livestock and other assets, thereby generating smooth, longer-term income (Islam and Pushkar 2012). This is no trivial help for a poor family, for whom a sudden dip in income can, in the absence of the availability of microloans, lead to a downward spiral into destitution. Various criticisms notwithstanding, microcredit certainly plays some valuable functions in the lives of poor people, a fact that is reflected in the briskly increasing demand for microcredit over the years in Bangladesh and elsewhere.

Next, we turn to the impact of non-microcredit activities of NGOs. In the past 40 years or so, Bangladesh has achieved remarkable improvements in health and social indicators—such as infant, under-five mortality and maternal mortality rates, fertility rate immunization coverage, and tuberculosis control; and gender disparity in education. These improvements took place notwithstanding the country's low per capita income, widespread poverty, weak health care and education systems, and low public spending on health and education. These achievements in health and social indicators are considered "exceptional" in the sense that they far exceed those expectations of a country at a similar level of income.

There is a good deal of consensus that much of this success owes to the efforts of the NGO sector of the country,[10] which relied on low-cost solutions, local innovation, and social mobilization to initiate and scale up those programs. In the health area, NGOs such as BRAC, Grameen, Ganoshathaya Kendra and Bangladesh Diabetic Samity have played leading roles in improving health outcomes of poor people in rural areas.

In this connection, some successes with NGO interventions is worth mentioning. In the 1970s, child mortality was rampant, partly due to diarrhea and partly due to six immunizable diseases. To overcome this challenge, BRAC, in 1979, collaborated with the government to implement the oral rehydration therapy program. This effort, which was later expanded to include immunization, and Vitamin-A supplementation, was joined by many other NGOs. By the 1990s, these interventions yielded a rich dividend of health outcomes, resulting in lower child mortality and a higher percentage of immunized children compared with other countries at similar income levels.

The treatment of tuberculosis is another success story. In 1993, NGOs, together with the government, initiated one of the world's most successful and innovative tuberculosis treatment, known as directly observed treatment, short course (DOTS). This program, which entailed mass deployment of community health workers by NGOs, was able to increase the number of people cured from less than 50 percent to more than 90 percent, which is among the highest in the developing world.

The final example relates to NGOs' role in popularizing contraceptive use. The role of female health workers from the NGOs was the key to success. By providing door-to-door family planning services, the country was able to overcome some social and cultural barriers associated with contraceptive use and achieve a high (exceeding 62 percent) contraceptive prevalence and a dramatic reduction in birth rates, from an average 6.9 births per woman in 1971 to 2.1 in 2016—an extraordinary achievement compared to countries with similar levels of development (Chowdhury and others 2013).

NGO programs have also made an important contribution toward achieving gender parity in primary education. While the primary education provided by the government had a wide reach, it still fell short of the target of reaching the poorest children in remote areas. Here, nonformal education provided by the NGOs—particularly by BRAC—filled an important lacuna. These no-frill schools usually have one classroom and one teacher and follow a schedule that suits students' convenience. Over the years, these efforts have helped achieve gender parity in enrollment by taking on board those who have been bypassed by the formal system.

What explains the apparent success of NGOs in the provision of social services, particularly in health and education? A number of explanations have been offered. First, Bangladesh adopted a pluralistic approach toward the provision of social services involving many stakeholders. Rather than sticking to a singular approach, NGOs and private enterprises worked in lockstep with the public sector, thereby creating a synergy of outcomes. Second, Bangladeshi NGOs undertook a trial-and-error method—always experimenting and course-correcting till they got their interventions right. NGOs in Bangladesh are well known for improvising context-specific innovative technologies and policies. This learning approach was a critical factor behind their success (Abed 2013).

Third, NGOs took a community-based approach, which is intensive among female workers. The use of female agency is cited as the key element in the story of the country's NGO-led social progress in health and education (Sen 2013). This approach of extensive female deployment has many advantages: it helps elicit greater cooperation from the potential beneficiaries, to increase the reach into the target population—more often deprived women and girls—and to broaden the impact of the intervention. This community-based approach deploying female workers has also had some social externalities—it contributes to improved social norms and attitudes regarding gender equality and female mobility in rural areas.

Finally, compared to government agencies, NGOs are generally more efficient, agile, and nimble—with deep access to the societal nooks and crannies of the country. This has also helped NGOs to make inroads into remote and underserved areas where the government, given its capacity constraint, is at a disadvantage to operate.

Conclusions

The four drivers of development emerged out of the fortuity of the 1970s—the garment industry from the MFA, the highly protective international trading regime governing the textile and apparel trade at that time; the international migration (and the consequent remittances) from the oil crisis that gripped the world after the Yum-Kippur war; agricultural productivity surge and the rise of the NGO sector out of the dire economic conditions that besieged post-war Bangladesh. While the advent of those drivers was sudden and unexpected, their survival and continued success was conditional on a set of favorable political economic factors that existed nationally and internationally.

In RMG, its business leaders have been successful, from the beginning, in harnessing political support behind their cause from the government, irrespective of its political hue. Indeed, many of these entrepreneurs have over time emerged as powerful political actors; 10 percent of the members of parliament in 2013 were RMG owners and still many others had indirect financial interests in the industry (Chambers 2013). Given this powerful influence on the government, this industry has been in a position to elicit maximum financial as well as regulatory favor from the government, so much so that it could flout minimum rights and safety of the workers.

In the case of international migration, the process is largely controlled by the migrant recruitment agencies. The leadership of this business has also been successful in garnering political support behind its cause—particularly, given the government's proclaimed objective of maximizing international labor migration and remittances. As in the case of the RMG industry, entrepreneurs of this industry have deep financial resources and are politically connected, many of them also being members of parliament. Given the confluence of economic interest with that of the government, this industry had also been successful in carving out a policy framework that has helped to maximize labor migration abroad without much of an effective safeguard for workers, either at home or abroad.

For agriculture—particularly for food—there is a broad-based support for its growth and sustenance both nationally and internationally. As the history of Bangladesh indicates, all governments, irrespective of party, have promoted agriculture. Other than altruism—empathy for the poorer segment of the society—this support is driven by enlightened self-interest: even the most popular government in Bangladesh would not survive in power if it failed to provide food to the people, a lesson that all governments have taken to heart. In addition, this domestic consensus has been supported by a strong international backing for agricultural development in the country. This is evident from the generous development assistance received from the international development community for agricultural development—for example, grants and loans, technology, and policy advice.

Finally, in the case of NGOs, the government has in general provided space and extended a supporting hand, being conscious of its own capacity limit to provide various social services to the people. In this connection, it may be recalled that the most famous NGO of Bangladesh, Grameen Bank, was created as a statutory body with public funds. (However, over the years, the relationship between the NGOs and the government has had ebbs and flows.) Also, critically important for the continued growth and sustenance was the strong support from the international development community in favor of NGOs, which have been characterized as the "favored child" of international development assistance (Hulme and Edward 1997). These days a significant segment of global development assistance is channeled through NGOs. Bangladesh is no exception.

This briefly delineates the national and international factors that undergirded the continued growth and dynamism of the four drivers of development in Bangladesh. The question that arises now is the following: How long will the drivers hold up? We will explore this question in the next chapter.

Notes

1. Tacit knowledge, as contrasted from explicit knowledge, is the kind of knowledge that is difficult to transfer from one person to another by means of written or verbal instructions. This knowledge can be defined as skills, ideas, and experiences that people acquire by doing things—such as riding a bike, playing the piano, or driving a car—that are not easily codified or easily expressed. This kind of knowledge is often transmitted through social networks; it is captured when the knowledge-holder joins a network or a community of practice (Polyani 1966).
2. In 1980, another South Korean firm, Youngone Corporation, entered into a joint venture with a Bangladeshi garment firm, Trexim Ltd., which contributed 51 percent of the equity of the new joint venture. This company, Youngones Bangladesh, exported its first consignment of padded and non-padded jackets to Sweden in December 1980 (Yunus and Yamagata 2012).
3. The initial bonded warehouse operation was further simplified over time. These simplifications included the government placing the bonded warehouse facility under custody of the factory owners, thereby replacing the earlier practice of it being controlled by customs officers; second, instituting the practice of Utilization Permits, which relied on paper calculations replacing the original system of carrying out a physical inspection.
4. The Accord on Fire and Building Safety in Bangladesh included more than 220 Western retailers and brands, mostly European. The Accord made a binding commitment to ensure that suppliers met fundamental safety standards and that it would buy garments at rates that allowed

factories to operate without cutting corners. The deal also empowered an independent inspectorate to stop brands from patronizing factories that do not operate safely. The Alliance for Bangladesh Worker Safety, on the other hand, included 29 large US brands and oversaw safety improvements in more than 600 factories (Kazmin 2018). The Alliance, however, did not make the kind of binding legal commitments like the Accord. In addition to these two, there is a third compliance initiative—a much less-rigorous one—launched with the assistance of the International Labor Organization (ILO) and run by the Bangladeshi government for factories that produce for non-Western countries like Turkey, Russia, and so on. Following these agreements, worker fatalities have fallen markedly in the past five years. When these agreements expire in 2018, both the government and the BGMEA want to discontinue the international agreements, claiming that the country has the capability to monitor safety itself. Recently, with the support of the ILO, the government has set up a Remediation Coordination Cell to address work safety issues.

5. The number of Bangladeshi asylum seekers in Europe had grown significantly over the years, from almost 6000 in 2008 to more than 17,000 in 2016. A plurality of these migrants veered toward Italy, which represented 28 percent of the total applications lodged in European countries in 2008, and 39 percent in 2016 (when 6665 Bangladeshi migrants applied for protection in Italy) (International Migration Organization 2017).
6. There are around 1000 registered private recruitment agencies in Bangladesh, mostly based in Dhaka. However, the actual recruitment process is largely handled through an army of subagents (*dalals*), exceeding more than 10,000, who plough through the entire country in search of potential migrants. The registered recruiting agencies are members of Bangladesh Association of International Recruiting Agencies (BAIRA), the association of recruiting agencies, an organization charged with the task of self-regulation of the recruitment agencies. The Bureau of Manpower, Employment, and Training (BMET), a government department under the Ministry of Expatriates' Welfare and Overseas Employment, is responsible for the entire migration process, including management of the process and ensuring the welfare of migrant workers.
7. Bangladesh has three principal rice crops: Aus, Aman (transplanted and broadcast varieties), and Boro. Aus is sown during summer and harvested around autumn; Aman is sown during the rainy season and harvested around winter; and Boro is sown during winter and harvested in summer.
8. BRAC has gone through successive redefinition of its mission and name changes. It was previously known as the Bangladesh Rehabilitation

Assistance Committee, then renamed the Bangladesh Rural Advancement Committee, and currently rechristened Building Resources Across Communities.

9. There has been a steady increase in NGO activities not only in Bangladesh but globally. In the arena of international development, NGOs have emerged as the "favored child" of official development agencies; with the perceived failures of governments, many view NGOs as a magic bullet to target and fix the problems of development. However, this is too much of a starry-eyed, romantic view, as NGOs are riddled with many challenges (Werker and Ahmed 2008).
10. While it is widely acknowledged that NGOs as a group promoted innovative solutions to address issues of poverty, unemployment, health, and education, causal evidence in this regard is limited.

References

Abed, Fazle. 2013. Bangladesh's Health Revolution. *The Lancet* 382: 2048–2049.

Abrar, C.R. 2017. Lowering the Costs of Migration. *The Daily Star*, February 23. https://www.thedailystar.net/drivers-economy/lowering-the-costs-migration-1364815. Accessed 9 Aug 2018.

Adams, R.H., and John Page. 2005. Do International Migration and Remittances Reduce Poverty in Developing Countries? *World Development* 33 (10): 1645–1669.

Ahmed, Raisuddin, and Steven Haggleblade. 2000. Introduction. In *Out of the Shadow of Famine: Evolving Food Markets and Food Policy*, ed. Raisuddin Ahmed, Steven Haggleblade, and Taufiq-e-Elahi Chowdury. Baltimore: Johns Hopkins University Press.

Applebaum, Richard, and Nelson Lichtenstein. 2016. Introduction. In *Achieving Workers Rights in the Global Economy*, ed. Richard Applebaum and Nelson Lichtenstein, 1–25. Ithaca: Cornell University Press.

Banerjee, Abhijeet, Dean Karlan, and Jonathan Zinmand. 2015. Six Randomized Evaluations of Microcredit: Introduction and Further Steps. *American Economic Journal: Applied Economics* 7: 1–21.

Bangladesh Financial Intelligence Unit. 2015. *NGO/NPO Sector Assessment of Bangladesh*. Dhaka: Bangladesh Financial Intelligent Unit.

BBS, Bangladesh Bureau of Statistics. 2014. *Report on Survey on the Use of Remittances*. Statistical Report. Dhaka: Government of Bangladesh.

BGMEA. 2018. Bangladesh Garment Manufacturers and Exporters Association. July 16. http://www.bgmea.com.bd/home/pages/tradeinformation.

BMET. 2018. Bureau of Manpower, Employment and Training. August 31. http://www.old.bmet.gov.bd/BMET/stattisticalDataAction. Accessed 14 Sept 2018.

BRAC. 2017. BRAC at a Glance. December. http://www.brac.net/sites/default/files/ataglance/BRAC-at-a-glance-Dec-2017e2.pdf. Accessed 31 Aug 2018.

Chambers, John. 2013. How Textile Kings Weave a Hold on Bangladesh. Dhaka, May 2. https://www.reuters.com/article/us-bangladesh-garments-special-report/special-report-how-textile-kings-weave-a-hold-on-bangladesh-idUSBRE9411CX20130503

Chowdhury, Mustaq, and others. 2013. The Bangladesh Paradox: Exceptional Health Achievement Despite Economic Poverty. *The Lancet* 382: 1734–1745.

Deb, Uttam. 2016. *Agricultural Transformations in Bangladesh: Extent, Drivers, and Implications.* Paper presented at the BAEA 15th Conference. Dhaka.

Desilver, Drew. 2018. Despite Talk of 'Trade War' with China, Highest U.S. Tariffs Are on Imports from Other Asian Countries. *Pew Research Center*, April 5. http://www.pewresearch.org/fact-tank/2018/04/05/despite-talk-of-trade-war-with-china-highest-u-s-tariffs-are-on-imports-from-other-asian-countries/. Accessed 10 Aug 2018.

Dhaka Tribune. 2017. Migrant Workers' Dreams End in Body Bags. December 18.

Dinh, Hinh, Thomas Rawski, Ali Zafar, Lihong Wang, and Eleonora Mavroeidi. 2013. *Tales from the Development Frontier.* Washington, DC: World Bank.

Economist. 2013. Feeding 1.36 Billion People Daily Bread. October 26. https://www.economist.com/china/2013/10/26/daily-bread. Accessed 15 Sept 2018.

———. 2017. Worries About Falling Remittances. June 8. Accessed 15 Sept 2018.

Faini, Riccardo. 2007. Remittances and the Brain Drain: Do More Skilled Migrants Remit More? *The World Bank Economic Review* 21 (1): 177–191.

Food and Agricultural Organization. 2014. FAO STATS: Online Database. Rome.

Grameen Bank. 2018. Grameen Bank: Introduction. January. http://www.grameen.com/introduction/. Accessed 3 Sept 2018.

Haeth, Rachel, and Mushfique Mobarak. 2015. Manufacturing Growth and the Lives of Bangladeshi Women. *Journal of Development Economics* 115: 1–15.

Hashemi, Syed, Sidney Schuler, and Ann Riley. 1996. Rural Credit Programs and Women's Empowerment in Bangladesh. *World Development* 24: 635–653.

Hulme, David, and Michael Edward. 1997. *NGOs, State and Donors: Too Close for Comfort?* London: Macmillan.

Hussain, Zahid. 2014. World Economic Forum. September 22. https://www.weforum.org/agenda/2014/09/remittances-multiplier-bangladesh-migration-labour/. Accessed 8 Aug 2018.

International Labor Organization. 2014. Wages in Asia and the Pacific: Dynamic but Uneven Progress. ILO Regional Office for Asia and the Pacific: Regional Economic and Social Analysis Unit (RESA). December. http://www.ilo.org/wcmsp5/groups/public/%2D%2D-asia/%2D%2D-ro-bangkok/%2D%2Dsro-bangkok/documents/publication/wcms_325219.pdf. Accessed 18 July 2018.

———. 2015. *Skilling the Workforce: Labour Migration and Skills Recognition and Certification*. Dhaka: International Labor Organization.

International Migration Organization. 2017. *Current Migration Trends from Bangladesh to Italy*. IOM Italy. Rome: International Migration Organization. Briefing: https://italy.iom.int/sites/default/files/documents/IOM_Italy_Briefing_01_Migration_trends_from_Bangladesh_to_Italy.pdf

Islam, Asadul, and Maitra Pushkar. 2012. Health Shocks and Consumption Smoothing in Rural Households: Does Microcredit Have a Role to Play? *Journal of Development Economics* 97 (2): 232–243.

Jaim, W.H.M., and Shaheen Akter. 2012. *Seed, Fertilizer and Innovations in Bangladesh: Industry and Policy Issues*. IFPRI Project Paper. Washington, DC: International Food Policy Research Institute.

Karim, Lamia. 2008. Demystifying Microcredit: The Grameen Bank, NGOs, and Neoliberalism in Bangladesh. *Cultural Dynamics* 20 (1): 5–29.

———. 2014. Analyzing Women's Empowerment: Microfinance and Garment Labor. *The Fletcher Forum of World Affairs* 38 (2): 153–166.

Kazmin, Amy. 2018. Rana Plaza Five Years on—Safety Is Greater but Not Guaranteed. *Financial Times*, April 23. https://www.ft.com/content/7ec413ec-46e6-11e8-8ee8-cae73aab7ccb

Khan, Mustaq. 2013. *The Political Settlement, Growth and Technical Progress in Bangladesh*. DIIS Working Paper 2013:01. London: DIIS Working Paper 2013:01.SOAS, London University.

Mascarenhas, Anthony. 1986. *Bangladesh: A Legacy of Blood*. London: Hodder & Stoughton.

NGO Affairs Bureau. 2018. NGO Affairs Bureau. July. http://www.ngoab.gov.bd/site/page/4623023a-745a-4593-8633-96c6cbda7f97/List-of-Local-NGOs. Accessed 4 Sept 2018.

Niimi, Yoko, Caglar Ozden, and Maurice Schiff. 2010. Remittances and the Brain Drain: Skilled Migrants Do Remit Less. *Annales d'Économie et de Statistique* 97/98: 123–142.

Osmani, S.R., Akhter Ahmed, Tahmeed Ahmed, Naomi Hossain, Saleemul Huq, and Asif Shahan. 2016. *Strategic Review of Food Security and Nutrition in Bangladesh*. Dhaka: World Food Program.

Pitt, M.M., and S.R. Khandker. 1998. The Impact of Group-based Credit on Poor households in Bangladesh: Does the Gender of Participants Matter? *Journal of Political Economy* 106 (5): 958–996.

Pitt, Mark, S.R. Khanker, and J. Cartwright. 2006. Empowering Women with Microfinance: Evidence from Bangladesh. *Economic Development and Cultural Change* 54 (4): 791–881.

Polyani, Michael. 1966. *The Tacit Dimension*. Chicago: University Press.

Rhee, Y.W. 1990. The Catalyst Model of Development: Lessons from Bangladesh's Success with Garments Exports. *World Development* 18 (2): 336–346.

Roodman, David, and Jonathan Morduch. 2014. The Impact of Microcredit on the Poor in Bangladesh: Revisiting the Evidence. *The Journal of Development Studies* 50 (4): 583–604.

Sen, Amartya. 2013. What's Happening in Bangladesh? *The Lancet* 382: 1966–1968.

The Daily Star. 2018. Tk 8000 a Month. September 14. Accessed 14 Oct 2018. https://www.thedailystar.net/business/news/bangladesh-rmg-garment-workers-minimum-salary-8000-takaannounced-1633342

United Nations. 2017. *International Migration Report 2017*. Annual. New York: United Nations.

USAID. 2015. *Food Security Country Framework for Bangladesh (FY 2015–2019)*. Washington, DC: FHI 360/FANTA.

Werker, Eric D., and Faisal Z. Ahmed. 2008. What Do Non-Governmental Organizations Do? *Journal of Economic Perspectives* 22 (2): 73–92.

World Bank. 1995. *Working with NGOs: A Practical Guide to Operational Collaboration Between the World Bank and Nongovernmental Organizations*. Operational Directive. Washington, DC: World Bank.

———. 2006. *Economics and Governance of Nongovernmental Organizations in Bangladesh*. Bangladesh Development Series, Paper 11. Washington, DC: World Bank.

———. 2012. *Bangladesh: Towards Accelerated, Inclusive and Sustainable Growth—Opportunities and Challenges (In Two Volumes) Volume II: Main Report*. Country Economic Report. Washington, DC: World Bank.

Yardley, Jim. 2013. Garment Trade Wields Power in Bangladesh. *New York Times*, July 24. https://www.nytimes.com/2013/07/25/world/asia/garment-trade-wields-power-in-bangladesh.html. Accessed 29 July 2018.

Yoshino, Naoyuki, Farhad Taghizadeh-Hesary, and Miyu Otsuka. 2017. *International Remittances and Poverty Reduction: Evidence from Asian Developing Countries*. Working Paper 759. Tokyo: Asian Development Bank Institute.

Yunus, Mohammad, and Tatsufumi Yamagata. 2012. The Garment Industry in Bangladesh. In *Dynamics of the Garment Industry in Low-Income Countries: Experience of Asia and Africa*, ed. Fukunishi Takahir, 1–28. Tokyo: IDE-JETRO.

CHAPTER 4

Risks and Challenges

Abstract Much of the recent growth and development in Bangladesh has been narrowly based; it has been primarily propelled by what is labeled in this study as the four drivers of development: ready-made garments; international migration and remittances: agriculture; and nongovernmental organizations. While these drivers have served the economy well in the past, their robustness is likely to be challenged in the future. This chapter identifies a trifecta of major risks, which are exogenous to the government and largely beyond its ability to manipulate. These are rooted, first, in the rapid changing technology in robotics and artificial intelligence; second, in the evolving global political and economic environment; and third, in climate change and natural disasters. Going forward, for sustained growth, the country needs to further diversify, which will require addressing various social, political, policy, and institutional challenges facing the economy, including poor governance, inadequate physical infrastructure, skill and educational bottlenecks, demographic burden, dwindling social capital, and lack of transformational leadership.

Keywords Automation • Climate change • Arabization • Grant financing

M. G. Quibria, *Bangladesh's Road to Long-term Economic Prosperity*, https://doi.org/10.1007/978-3-030-11587-6_4

Introduction

Bangladesh has achieved considerable economic progress in the last quarter century—it has transitioned from a highly vulnerable, low-income country to a relatively more stable lower-middle-income country, as per the World Bank classification. In the next quarter century, it seeks to achieve an even higher economic target—that of attaining the status of a high-income (developed) country; if realized, that would definitely be exceptional by the post-war international standards.[1] The road to high-income economy status is never smooth—it is paved with many obstacles, including the so-called middle-income trap.[2] This chapter seeks to explore how likely such a target is for Bangladesh, given the various risks and challenges associated with its development trajectory.

As we have argued in the preceding chapter, the country's current development dynamics is primarily determined by four drivers of development: ready-made garments (RMG), labor migration and remittances, agriculture, and nongovernmental organizations (NGO). The robustness of a long-term trajectory of the economy will be contingent on the continued strength of these four drivers of development as well as on the success of the economy in diversifying into new areas of manufacturing and services.

This chapter, however, envisages that going forward, there will be a constellation of exogenous risks—associated with changes in technology and the international economy, as well as environment and climatic factors—that will challenge the durability of the current drivers of development. In addition, the prospects of the emergence of new nodes of growth will be significantly muted—unless there are severe course corrections—by the existing constraints of policies, institutions, and infrastructure.

Risks

This section discusses the various risks that will face the economy. These risks relate to changes in technology in the case of RMG; developments in the international economy affecting migration and remittances; the impact of environmental and climatic changes in agriculture; and a combination of factors, both external and internal, in the case of NGOs.

Ready-made Garments

The world is experiencing a rapid technological revolution in robotics and artificial intelligence, a revolution that has been heralded as the fourth Industrial Revolution—or Industry 4.0. Recent research suggests that potential for automation seems to be higher in manufacturing than service sector jobs, which typically require more creative thinking or face-to-face interaction. This poses a concern for developing countries, which have large pools of low-skilled labor working in labor-intensive manufacturing.[3]

Most manufacturing activities, which are routine, repetitive, and codifiable, are in the bull's eye of the automation revolution. This automation has already disrupted many industries, displacing labor and reshoring factories from overseas. Recent years provide some examples. More than two-thirds of robots now inhabit the automotive, electrical/electronics, and metal and machinery industries, where the adverse employment effect has been most severe. Foxconn Technology Group, which is based in China, is the world's largest electronics assembler; it cut its workforce by 30 percent by introducing robots into the production process. In 2017, 3D printing technologies enabled the German company Adidas AG to establish two "speed factories" for shoe production—one in Ansbach, Germany, and the other in Atlanta in the United States—eliminating more than 1000 jobs in Vietnam. In 2012, the Dutch multinational technology company Philips Electronics shifted production from China back to the Netherlands (Hallward-Driemeird and Nayyar 2018).

A recent report by the International Labor Organization warned that 137 million workers—or 56 percent of the workforces in Cambodia, Indonesia, the Philippines, Thailand, and Vietnam—were at high risk of losing their jobs to automation—with those in the garment industry being particularly vulnerable (International Labor Organization 2016).

The apparel industry, which has curiously defied automation for a long time since the invention of the sewing machine, is now on the cusp of a new wave of automation. The apparent barrier to automation in sewing had been the nature of the fabric itself—it's flexible, it stretches, it warps, and it folds. In short, robots are clumsy at handling soft, flexible material. This characteristic of the fabric apparently led William J. Bank, president of the Blue Jeans Corporation, to famously predict in 1970 that there would be a man on Mars before the production of apparel was automated.

It seems that about half a century later, Bank is about to be proven wrong and recent developments in sewing technology—such as Sewbo or

Sewbot—have largely addressed the problems that defied automation. Sewbot, which was many years in development with financial support from Walmart and the US Department of Defense, is currently on stream. These robots can already make simple items like pillows and bath mats on a commercial scale. In 2018, the company plans to offer a T-shirt production line. One robotic sewing line can replace a conventional line of ten workers and produce about 1142 T-shirts in an eight-hour period, compared to just 669 for the human sewing line. Alternatively, the robot, working under the guidance of a single human handler, can make as many T-shirts per hour as 17 human workers (Quartz 2017).

An immediate response to this development was the relocation of a Chinese garments firm. In 2018, Tianyuan Garments Company, whose products include brands such as Adidas and Armani, decided to invest $20 million in a 100,000 square foot factory in Little Rock, Arkansas. Staffed with 21 robotic production lines, the company will be capable of making 1.2 million T-shirts a year. Typically, manufacturing in the United States is much more expensive than producing in China because of the former's higher labor costs. However, in a completely automated production line, labor cost shrinks to about $0.33 per shirt. To produce a similar denim shirt in Bangladesh, it costs about $0.22 in labor, according to an estimate from the Institute for Global Labor and Human Rights. That same labor would cost $7.47 in the United States, putting the labor cost for Tianyuan Garments' American-made shirt almost at par with Bangladesh, one of the cheapest labor markets in the world. By producing in the United States, the Chinese company also hopes to shorten the geographical distance between production and consumption (Quartz 2017).

It may be noted here that other than productivity and profitability, the advantage of utilizing robots in the apparel industry is that they can handle the intricacies of manufacturing in ways humans cannot and improve the quality of goods when the demand for standards is high and rising. Besides, it places production in the geographical proximity of consumers, opening future opportunities for made-to-order manufacturing. However, the present cost/benefit calculus of deploying robots vis-à-vis the existing labor-intensive manufacturing in developing countries tends to favor the latter. In the future, as the costs of robots decrease and wages rise in developing countries, many industry analysts believe that the cost/benefit ratio is likely to flip the other way.

How will this development affect the long-term prospects of the RMG industry, which has been the cornerstone of Bangladesh's manufacturing and exports? The technological innovations associated with Sewbot and other similar machines are in their infancy—and have not yet disrupted the global apparel industry. The question is not whether it will happen, but when. When this happens, it will have devastating economic ramifications for Bangladesh as well as other RMG-exporting countries.

However, in recent years, the Bangladesh RMG sector has also gone through some restructuring to incorporate automation to fortify their competitive position. According to a recent *Wall Street Journal* report, major Bangladeshi factories had already introduced such items as automatic knitting machines, replacing manual knitting for knit sweaters production, and automatic laser finishing machines for jeans, replacing the traditional methods of denim finishing like sandblasting and stone washing. The unfortunate outcome has been that many smaller factories that could not afford such new technologies have gone under. Although these automation measures had increased efficiency, this efficiency was achieved at some costs—by displacing workers. Consequently, the pace of job growth in the garment and textile sector has declined to 60,000 a year from over 300,000 annually between 2003 and 2010, as per World Bank data (*The Wall Street Journal* 2018).

The RMG sector in Bangladesh is now confronted with a double squeeze from both supply and demand sides: on the supply side, there is increasing competition from the low-cost producers of East Africa and, on the demand side, as transmitted by retailers, there are rising expectations of international consumers for low prices for "fast fashion". This double-squeeze resulted in a decline in prices offered to garment producers. Data suggest that since 2013, the amount paid by lead firms to Bangladeshi supplier factories had declined on average by 13 percent. The cause of this decline was not linked either to the price of cotton or exchange rate fluctuations, but to a retailer and brand-pricing squeeze on supplier factories (Anner 2018). In response to this squeeze, the country's biggest clothing producers had already started to adopt automation as a cost-saving strategy (*The Wall Street Journal* 2018).

As wages move up and newer and more efficient machines of automation come on stream, there is likely to reach an inflection point that may mark the end of the country's comparative advantage in low-value-added RMG. This is an alarming prospect that confronts not only Bangladesh but also many developing countries that envisioned a path to economic development through labor-intensive manufacturing—as many East Asian countries successfully did in the past. This frightful scenario has been labeled "premature deindustrialization" by Harvard economist Dani Rodrik. Currently, many developing countries are experiencing a decline in manufacturing at levels of income that are a fraction of those at which the advanced economies started to deindustrialize. This deindustrialization is more pronounced concerning employment than output. In the face of the current onslaught of labor-saving technological progress, many countries would run out of industrialization opportunities sooner and at much lower levels of income compared to the experience of early industrializers (Rodrik 2016).

If the current manufacturing phase is abruptly curtailed, some economists argue that Bangladesh, as well as other countries in South Asia, should focus on services. The premise of this argument is that the global labor market is being increasingly integrated, and many services can be provided digitally across the Internet. However, the relevant question is the following: Can the Bangladeshi workers make a successful entry into the global service trade on a large scale? Prima facie, the profile of Bangladeshi workers, with their education and skills level, does not make one particularly optimistic about this prospect. We discuss this further in a forthcoming section.

Migration and Remittances

With rising economic nationalism and aversion to immigrant workers, the halcyon days of ever-expanding labor export seem to be almost over. Although Bangladeshi workers have often encountered occasional bans in the Gulf countries as well as Southeast Asian economies, these restrictions may become increasingly tighter in the future. As Western countries never had a guest worker program for Bangladeshi workers, the entry of Bangladeshi nationals to those countries, by regular and irregular means, has also become increasingly difficult with growing anti-immigrant sentiment, the latest example being the cancellation in the United States of the diversity program that allowed entry of a significant number of Bangladeshis into the country.

However, for purposes of international migration and remittances, the most significant restrictions are those that have been placed in the Gulf countries through various labor market indigenization programs, the most important being Saudization—the Nitaqat program—a plan to replace foreign workers by Saudi workers. The program has stringent quantitative targets for private companies to employ Saudi nationals, violation of which results in a severe penalty, including debarment from government contracts, and hefty taxes on imports of foreign workers, when permitted (International Monetary Fund 2018).

This Saudization program, however, is not new. It began in 2011 as part of a government initiative to encourage employment of Saudi nationals in the private sector. However, this nationalization policy gained more momentum after Saudi Arabia's oil economy began to shrink with the plummeting of crude prices in 2014. Despite its being the world's largest oil exporter, Saudi Arabia's current government expenditures now outstrip oil revenues, a deficit which is projected to continue till 2023. In 2018, the budget deficit amounted to about 8 percent of GDP, which was met by drawing down the foreign currency reserves as well as by foreign borrowing.

In 2016, the country initiated its 2030 vision; an important element of that vision included the vigorous pursuit of the Saudization program. In recent years, Saudi unemployment has spiked, particularly of youth and females. The Saudi "nationalization policy" is aimed at boosting Saudi participation in private sector jobs to reduce the dependence of its citizens on government dole-outs and to pare down the public-sector wage bill, which accounts for about half of all government expenditure. Most Saudi nationals—almost two-thirds—are employed by the government (International Monetary Fund 2018).

The Saudi government has taken a two-pronged approach to its Saudization program. The first is to "nationalize" specific industries in the private sector by limiting employment—including the complete ban of foreign workers in some retail business activities (e.g., gold and jewelry, mobile phone, and electrical shops). The private sector businesses that violate the government quotas regarding employment of expatriate workers are subject to substantial penalty. The second is to make it more expensive for migrant workers to live and remain in the kingdom—by levying a relatively large fee on guest workers and their dependents (these fees were further increased in 2018). The outcome of this two-pronged program has been a massive exodus of foreign workers, more than 800,000, from the country since 2017 (*Daily Mail* 2018).

Saudi Arabia hosts the largest number of Bangladeshi migrant workers and is the most important source of foreign remittances. Considering the restrictions imposed in the Nitaqat program, prospects for employment of Bangladeshi workers in the private sector are fast shrinking. The only exception in this regard is the domestic household workers who are exempt from the Nitaqat quotas or the levies on foreign workers. However, these workers earn the lowest wages of all categories of workers and have been subject to various abuses, including torture, as is widely reported in Bangladesh and international national media.

Following the Saudi lead, other Gulf countries have adopted policies like those of Saudi Arabia. Labeled variously as Emiratization, Kuwaitization, Qatarization, and Omanization, these policies have not been as vigorous or as effective as the Nitaqat program of Saudi Arabia. If the oil crunch continues, the push to further restrict foreign workers will continue. Now, some Gulf countries are also contemplating other restrictive policies, including the imposition of taxes on migrants' remittances and enforcement of a maximum stay in the host country. In any event, the period of mass influx of migrant workers to the Gulf countries may come to an end sooner rather than later.

Agriculture[4]

The third risk relates to agriculture, which has done a stupendous job of feeding the expanding population, much beyond the early prognostications of most analysts. Nevertheless, the potential for continuous future expansion of agricultural productivity is not necessarily assured, as future growth in productivity will depend on many factors, including the more intensive use of the existing higher-yield seed and fertilizer technology and on further technological progress. While technology will be critical, so will be the role of natural and environmental factors for determining the country's future ability to produce food.

Bangladesh loses agriculture land at no less than 1 percent per year due to reasons that include urbanization, human settlement, road infrastructure, waterlogging, depletion of groundwater, and soil fertility, erosion, and salinity. This would suggest that the country would lose at least one-quarter of its land in the next 30 years (Rashid 2014). In the past three decades, the country suffered loss in not only quantity but quality of land. This loss in quality stemmed from a number of sources. First, during this period, 840,000 ha of agricultural land was degraded by increased salinity. The main factors behind this salinity intrusion include sea-level rise, surge in cyclones and storms, and increased shrimp culture. Second, soil fertility degradation adversely affected 8 million ha of agricultural land. It occurred due to imbalance in fertilizer use (overuse of subsidized nitrogen fertilizers) and intensification of crop cultivation, and the advance of monoculture rice without rotation. In the past, most farmers overused nitrogen fertilizer, neglecting to combine it with a balanced dose of phosphate and potassium fertilizer along with micronutrient application.[5] Third, river-bank erosion—which results in washing away of topsoil and depositing sands on the croplands from upstream—accounted for about 40 percent of land degradation. Every year about 1200 km of riverbanks, primarily of the Padma, Jamuna, and Meghna, are faced with erosion-related problems. These rivers, which combine and empty into the Bay of Bengal at the Meghna estuary, devour thousands of hectares of floodplain, making thousands of people landless and homeless every year. This problem of riverbank erosion is likely to get worse with the further rise in the river water flows, following increased melting of ice in the Himalayas due to climate change (Government of Bangladesh and FAO 2011).

Continuous land loss, in conjunction with population growth, explains the dwindling farm size, which decreased from 0.81 to 0.51 ha between 1984 and 2008. Bangladesh's farm size, as expected, is among the smallest in the world.

Bangladesh's geographical location—at the head of the Bay of Bengal, astride the largest river delta on Earth—land characteristics, and climate make it extremely vulnerable to natural and human-induced hazards. Maplecroft, a leading global risk analytics firm, identified 32 "extreme risk" countries in its Climate Change Vulnerability Index (CCVI), which evaluated the sensitivity of populations, the physical exposure of countries, and governmental capacity to adapt to climate change over the next 30 years. Bangladesh ranked first in the 2014 index, implying that it would likely suffer the most from climate change by 2025 compared to any other country (Maplecroft 2014). Rainfall is expected to increase by 10–15 percent during the monsoon season by 2030 and by 27 percent by 2075; rising sea level is expected to inundate 120,000 km^2 by 2050; 14 percent more of the country would become extremely prone to floods by 2030; cyclones in the Bay of Bengal would occur more frequently due to increasing temperature, and the peak intensity of hurricanes would increase by 5–10 percent. Coastal salinity problems are likely to exacerbate as changing rain patterns reduce the amount of dry season water supply from upstream river sources.

Overall, crop production would suffer by 30 percent by the end of the century whereas rice production would fall by 8 percent and wheat production by 32 percent by 2050 (FPMU 2013). Winter crop production would be severely affected by a warmer and drier environment during non-monsoon seasons, while moisture stress might force farmers to reduce the area under irrigation.

In short, if climate change continues unabated, the plight of Bangladesh will be grim. If the sea level predictions are correct, parts of the country may disappear. Nearly one-quarter of Bangladesh is less than 7 feet above sea level; two-thirds are less than 15 feet above sea level. So rising seas coupled with storm surges could put large parts of the population and agricultural land under the threat of severe flooding. If that happens, the economic toll would be catastrophic, with much of the economic gains achieved in the past decades, including in food–population balance, simply evaporating. However, in recent years, with both domestic and international resources, Bangladesh has made considerable investments in projects aimed at mitigating and adapting to climate change. Yet, these investments are not sufficient to address the existing risks, let alone the future risks from climate change. Besides the lack of adequate international funding, these efforts were also hamstrung by domestic implementation capacity (Government of Bangladesh 2015).

Nongovernmental Organizations

We make some brief remarks about the risks associated with the NGOs' contribution to growth going forward.

First, as the World Bank notes, most NGOs in Bangladesh face some of the governance issues associated with the country's for-profit sector; they tend to be founder-dominated and typically governed by the founder's friends and family (World Bank 2006). While this may have worked well with the first generation of NGOs, this mode of family-based governance would likely encounter new challenges going forward with the changing external environments. In addition, some of the founders of these NGOs—such as Abed and Yunus—are visionaries, outstanding social entrepreneurs, sui generis in their talents; in their absence, many of these organizations may run out of steam and face the real prospect of losing dynamism and innovativeness.

Second, as we have noted in an earlier chapter, NGOs are heavily dependent on foreign financing, particularly in their non-microfinance activities. These activities, which are primarily underwritten by international grants, are likely to face a crunch going forward, as the country graduates from its status as Least Developed Country (LDC) and, with it, much of grant financing might diminish or evaporate. In the absence of domestic funding from philanthropy (which has been mostly absent so far), many NGOs are likely to face an existential crisis.

Finally, as noted earlier, NGOs have made a noteworthy contribution toward improving the health and educational indicators of the poor segments of the society. Concerning health, the contribution was related mainly to addressing the first generation of poverty-linked infectious, nutritional, and maternity-related diseases. However, given the epidemiological transition, future efforts will need to treat chronic noncommunicable diseases—for example, cardiovascular diseases (like heart attacks and stroke), cancers, chronic respiratory diseases (like chronic obstructive pulmonary disease and asthma), and diabetes—which would require, among others, more intensive use of clinician resources (i.e., primary care physicians and nurses). In the absence of adequate clinical resources, future NGO efforts are likely to be much circumscribed in scope and be subject to serious diminishing returns.

Challenges

In addition to these factors, the country faces many intractable challenges, which include poor governance, infrastructural bottlenecks, non-inclusive institutions, dwindling social capital, and myopic leadership.

Poor Governance

Poor governance is a grave challenge for Bangladesh (Islam 2014).

Misgovernance is often used in a narrow sense to imply corruption. If that narrow definition is used, Bangladesh has an abundance of it in every sphere of life. It has been corroborated by a recent 2018 national survey of more than 15,000 households which reported that the majority of those sampled fell prey to some form of corruption in obtaining services from both public and private sectors. Law enforcement agencies (police) were rated as the most corrupt among the 18 services included in the study, followed by passport offices and Bangladesh Road Transport Authority (Transparency International Bangladesh 2018).

Besides petty corruption, major corruption exists in the government, even in areas that were previously considered sacrosanct such as bribes for public-sector jobs; a minister of the government resigned a few years ago following bribery allegations—amounting to $86,000—from applicants seeking jobs on the state-run railway (BBC 2012). Though corruption is widespread in public-sector employment, the nature of corruption seems to vary between jobs. In the higher echelons of the government, rather than outright bribery, the more salient form of corruption is political: it is party affiliation rather than merit that determines the recruitment and promotion of bureaucrats. Besides patronage and rent distribution, this practice, which applies across all regimes, is, of course, related to a strategy of regime maintenance (Khan 2017).

In the areas of procurements and contracts, corruption is also rampant. According to the World Bank's Enterprise Survey, 49 percent of firms expected to give gifts to secure a contract (World Bank 2013). This appears to have become a standard operating procedure, so much so that it has allegedly percolated even into international contracts. A related incident in this regard concerns the cancellation of a concessional loan by the World Bank, amounting to $1.2 billion, to build the country's longest bridge over the Padma, citing concerns of corruption. However, in 2017, the Canadian court found no proof of the Padma bridge bribery conspiracy and the Ontario Superior Court acquitted ex-SNC-Lavalin executives (allegedly the involved party with the government officials) and dismissed the case. It is apparent that the World Bank and the Canadian court held different evidentiary standards to prosecute a case (*The Wall Street Journal* 2012).

Newspapers also abound with reports of the larcenies of various kinds and magnitudes in the financial sector involving high-level bank officials. Irregularities are more common and the financial magnitudes are larger in the state-owned banks, where government controls are more direct.[6] According to a *New York Times* report, between 2010 and 2012, one of the largest state-owned banks, Sonali Bank, illegally gave out $454 million in loans, including nearly $344 million to Hallmark Group, a textile business, which connived with a branch manager to issue fraudulent letters of credit to fictitious companies. Another $565 million in bank assets were said to have been defrauded from the state-owned BASIC Bank between 2009 and 2012 allegedly in connivance with senior bank officials (*New York Times* 2016).

These scams are not confined only to these state-owned banks; they seem to have affected the operations of the private banks as well. Recent years have seen the proliferation of nonperforming loans in the banking sector, much of which is owed to private banks, whose owners happen to be owner-directors of the respective banks. It is alleged that there is an "odious nexus" between owner-directors of private banks who borrow from each other's banks with no intention of paying them back at all (*The Daily Star* 2018).

Corruption is essentially a covert activity, most of which escapes public attention. The perception-based indicators of corruption are one way to gauge the extent of corruption in a country. Transparency International publishes an annual Corruption Perception Index which ranks countries according to the extent to which corruption is believed to exist.[7] Bangladesh has consistently ranked low in position—in the lowest quartile of countries—over the years. In 2017, it was placed at 143 among 180 countries ranked, lower than India, Pakistan, Nepal, and Myanmar. This ranking does not, of course, provide a resounding testament to the state of the country's governance.

Governance is, however, more than corruption. Governance is a multidimensional concept that federates many aspects of governing. One such composite index is provided by Worldwide Governance Indicators (WGI) of governance, which has emerged as the industry leader. The WGI cover more than 200 countries and present information on six aggregate indicators: voice and accountability; government effectiveness; political stability and absence of violence; regulatory quality; rule of law; and control of corruption.

Voice and accountability consider various aspects of the political process, civil liberties, and political rights. Government effectiveness incorporates measures on the quality of public service provision, the quality of bureaucracy, the insulation of the civil service from political pressures, and the credibility of the government's commitment to policies. Political stability and absence of violence measure the likelihood that the government may be overthrown or destabilized by unconstitutional means, including politically motivated violence or terrorism. Regulatory quality measures the incidence of market-friendly policies and the burdens from excessive regulations. Rule of law includes indicators that gauge the confidence of the agents in—and their compliance with—the rules of society. The final set of indicators measures the perception of corruption in the government.[8]

The governance estimate for each aggregate indicator is derived from individual sources in each period and is normalized so that it has a mean of 0 and standard deviation of 1. This means that virtually all the scores lie between −2.5 and 2.5, and the aggregate indicators are measures of relative performances of a country in a period (the higher the score of a country, the better is its performance concerning governance).

Table 4.1 provides a comparative analysis of the quality of governance between India and Bangladesh. It shows that Bangladesh performs worse than India in all indicators of governance. Bangladesh also fares worse than the global average in all indicators of governance. Finally, data also suggest (but are not exhibited in the table) that Bangladesh ranks worse than the average for low-middle-income countries in all indicators of governance.

Notwithstanding the dismal record in governance, the country has performed well in the past, primarily, as was argued earlier, because of the robust performance of the four drivers of development, which were shielded from the ravages of misgovernance for broad political–economic reasons. However, going forward, if the drivers lose their momentum, it will be increasingly critical to improve the quality of governance across the board to sustain the present trajectory of growth.

Table 4.1 Indicators of governance: Bangladesh and India 2016

Governance indicators	*Bangladesh*	*India*
Control of corruption: Estimate	−0.8	−0.3
Control of corruption: Percentile rank	21.2	47.1
Government effectiveness: Estimate	−0.7	0.1
Government effectiveness: Percentile rank	25.5	57.2
Political stability and absence of violence/terrorism: Estimate	−1.2	−1
Political stability and absence of violence/terrorism: Percentile rank	10.5	14.3
Regulatory quality: Estimate	−0.8	−0.3
Regulatory quality: Percentile rank	22.1	41.3
Rule of law: Estimate	−0.6	−0.1
Rule of law: Percentile rank	30.8	52.4
Voice and accountability: Estimate	−0.6	0.4
Voice and accountability: Percentile Rank	31	58.6

Source: World Bank Database

Note: The governance estimate for each aggregate indicator is normalized so that it has a mean of 0 and standard deviation of 1. This means that virtually all the scores lie between −2.5 and 2.5, and the aggregate indicators are measures of relative performance of a country in a particular period

Finally, it may be noted in passing that the importance of good governance is particularly crucial for a resource-poor country like Bangladesh, which has few resources to waste. If misgovernance results in auctioning of jobs, it leads to misallocation of human resources—the talented end up in dead-end jobs and the deadbeat end up in challenging leadership positions—and results in tremendous waste for the economy.

It is often argued that much of the economic success of Singapore can be traced to its meritocracy, which has been a core principle of governance in Singapore. The country has devised an excellent education system and a meritocratic mechanism to allocate talents to where they are needed the most in the society. An analogous principle also applies to the allocation of financial capital. Resources flow where they can be most efficiently utilized. Subversion of this principle leads to crony capitalism—misallocation of financial resources to those who are politically connected, and not to those who can make the best use of those resources—and growth suffers, as the past experiences of many Asian and African countries will attest. Finally, investments in good governance should be viewed as a down payment for the flow of future foreign direct investments; good governance—which ensures the rule of law, effective and clean government, and political stability—can be a tremendous magnet for attracting foreign investments in a resource-poor country, as the history of Singapore amply demonstrates.

If Bangladesh aspires to be like Singapore in growth and development, it needs to aspire to the level of good governance that Singapore achieved.

Infrastructure Bottlenecks

Infrastructure—such as roads, railroads, ports, electricity, telecommunications, and water supply and sanitation—is critical for economic development. Starting virtually from scratch, Bangladesh has made considerable progress since its independence in its infrastructure development—including investing in some multi-billion-dollar infrastructure projects such as the Jamuna Bridge and the Padma Bridge, the former having been completed in 1998 while the latter's construction is well under way. Notwithstanding these improvements, the state of infrastructure in the country remains quite inadequate vis-à-vis its requirements. Table 4.2, which is taken from the Global Competitiveness Report, provides a comparative picture of the state of infrastructure of Bangladesh and other South Asian countries. It may be noted that all South Asian countries rank low relative to other economies in the world. Even within South Asia, Bangladesh fares poorly. Needless to state, poor infrastructure has implications not only for citizens' welfare but also for costs of production, transportation, and international competitiveness.

Nowhere is the problem of infrastructure deficit more starkly manifested than in Dhaka, the capital city that accounts for 35 percent of Bangladesh's GDP and is home to most of the country's manufacturing, government, business, healthcare, and educational institutions. With a

Table 4.2 State of infrastructure in South Asia: 2017–2018

Country		*Infrastructure*	*Roads*	*Rail transport*	*Port*	*Air transport*	*Electricity*
		Overall					
Bangladesh	Rank/137	116	105	60	85	115	101
	Value	2.9	3.1	2.9	3.6	3.3	3.7
India	Rank/137	46	55	28	4.7	61	80
	Value	4.6	4.3	4.4	4.6	4.6	4.7
Pakistan	Rank/137	82	76	52	73	91	115
	Value	3.8	3.9	3.3	4	4	2.9
Sri Lanka	Rank/137	79	61	55	57	75	96
	Value	3.9	4.2	3.2	4.5	4.2	4

Source: World Economic Forum: The Global Competitiveness Report 2017–2018

Note: Values are on a 1–7 scale unless indicated otherwise

population of more than 18 million (UN 2016), it is also the most crowded city in the world. Often rated as one of the least livable cities, it has about 3.5 million people who live in informal settlements that lack essential services and access to infrastructure.

In the absence of efficient traffic management and a public mass rapid transit system, millions of city dwellers rely on a woefully poor road infrastructure. Roads cover just 7 percent of the city, compared with around 25 percent of Paris and Vienna and 40 percent of Washington and Chicago, according to one analysis. Dhaka also suffers from the absence of a planned road network, feeder streets leading to arterials leading to highways. There are 650 major intersections, but only 60 traffic lights, many of which do not work much of the time. Finally, Dhaka has too few sidewalks, and even those that exist are often impassable, as they are occupied by vendors and masses of poor citizens who make the curbside their home (Hobbs 2014).

Due to unprecedented road congestion, the average driving speed has dropped from 21 km per hour 10 years ago to less than 7 km per hour today. Continuing current trends—with more than 37,000 cars added to Dhaka streets every year—would result in a further slowdown of speed to 4 km an hour, slower than average walking pace! Congestion, which takes up 3.2 million working hours each day, costs the economy billions of dollars every year and deprives the city and the country of some of the most important potential economic benefits that could have resulted from urbanization (Fan and Rama 2017).

Poor road quality and congestion is not merely a Dhaka problem. It is a national problem. This is reflected in the many road accidents and deaths that happen every day. According to the National Committee to Protect Shipping, Roads and Railways (NCPSRR), an NGO which compiles road accident statistics based on newspaper reports, in 2017 at least 4284 people, including 516 women and 539 children, were killed (one of the highest in the world) and 9112 others injured in 3472 road accidents across Bangladesh (*Dhaka Tribune* 2018).

Poor roads are deadly to individuals and detrimental to the economy insofar as it slows down the wheels of the economy. Along with roads, ports are another critical ingredient of a dynamic open economy: if the roads are congested and the ports are blocked, it is then difficult to sustain a strategy of outward-oriented growth.

Chittagong is the principal seaport, which handles more than 90 percent of total external trade. Though the port has experienced exponential expansion in its operation, it has seen little growth in its infrastructural capacity (such as berth capacity and crane availability), leading to excessive vessel congestion, undue delay in unloading, lack of security, corruption, and so on.

The poor state of the port performance is reflected in the World Bank's logistics performance index for 2018. In the case of infrastructure, Bangladesh ranks at 109 among 167 countries. However, the aggregate indicator includes more than trade and transport indicators. It is a weighted average of the country scores on six indicators: efficiency of the clearance process—that is, speed, simplicity, and predictability of formalities; quality of trade- and transport-related infrastructure—for example, ports, railroads, roads, information technology; ease of arranging competitively priced shipments; competence and quality of logistics services—for example, transport operators, customs brokers; ability to track and trace consignments; and timeliness of shipments in reaching destination. In the overall raking, Bangladesh is placed at 100, below all South Asian countries except for the landlocked countries such as Nepal, Bhutan, and Afghanistan. Other than overall ranking, Bangladesh has also gone down in four areas of assessment—customs, infrastructure, ease of arranging shipping, and quality of logistics services—from the last survey. The country needs to make serious investments in its port and trade-related logistics to support its goal of further accelerating growth in future.

Part of the problem stems from underinvestment in infrastructure in the past. According to the Asian Development Bank, the previous average infrastructure investment (including both central government and private sector) in Bangladesh was about 1.7 percent of its GDP; as a percentage of GDP, this is one-fourth of China's (6.8 percent), less than one-third of Vietnam's (5.7 percent) and India's (5.4 percent), and about three-quarters of that of Indonesia (2.6 percent) and the Philippines (2.3 percent) (Asian Development Bank 2017). If Bangladesh wants to overcome its infrastructure deficit and sustain its growth trajectory, it must significantly boost its investments in infrastructure.

Non-inclusive Institutions

Drawing on contemporary and historical examples, Harvard economics professor Daron Acemoglu and Chicago political science professor James Robinson, in their recent magnum opus *Why Nations Fail*, argue that the key to enduring prosperity is "inclusive" institutions. They contend that when political and economic institutions are inclusive—which afford equal opportunity to all individuals to participate in societal affairs—they generate enduring prosperity for the nation. By inclusivity, Acemoglu and

Robinson envisage an institutional framework where the state creates incentives for people to invest and innovate by guaranteeing private property rights and enforcing contracts. The state also enables investment and growth by providing education and infrastructure. They contrast inclusive institutions with extractive institutions. These extractive institutions are the product of a political system in which the state is monopolized by a small elite that creates private gains for elites, often by impoverishing the broader society (Acemoglu and Robinson 2013).

According to the Acemoglu–Robinson perspective, politics is paramount to the creation and sustenance of institutions. Inclusive political institutions have two separate components: pluralism and political centralization. The former relates to the broad distribution of political power and participation, constraints and checks on politicians, and rule of law (participatory democracy). The latter refers to the monopoly of legitimate violence over a territory[9] and the ability of the state to regulate economic activity, impose taxes, and provide public goods. Extractive institutions arise when either of the two conditions fails to exist.

While this analysis emphasizes the salience of inclusive political institutions for long-term economic prosperity, it is not particularly insightful as a tool for analyzing contemporary developing-country political institutions, which are often imperfect and hybrid. To our interest, Mushtaq Khan (Khan 2017) has provided a more granular analysis of the state of political and economic institutions in Bangladesh—or what he calls the "political settlement" that looks at the distribution of power across political and economic organizations. According to Khan, the first phase of the country, 1971–1975, was characterized by a dominant party turning into a *vulnerable authoritarianism*. This period included an attempt at socialist planning based on nationalizing the manufacturing sector. Despite the enormous personal popularity of the father of the nation, his party failed to manage internal political competition, thus leading to the creation of a one-party state as a way of imposing discipline on its supporters. This *vulnerable authoritarianism* was unpopular and succumbed to a political coup.

The second phase, 1975–1990, saw the managed return to multiparty politics under political parties led by military rulers. According to Khan, this represents a hybrid period, with characteristics of both *vulnerable authoritarianism* and *competitive clientelism*. This period allowed multiparty democracy with some authoritarian limits on the extent of political competition.

The third phase, 1990–2006, was characterized by *competitive clientelism* where shaky political institutions were in equilibrium with the competitive clientelist distribution of power. During this period, all powerful political factions had a reasonable chance of obtaining power and accessing political rents. This created a measure of investor confidence in the long-term stability of the political system.

The fourth phase, beginning with 2008, saw the evolution of the system from *competitive clientelism* to an effective one-party system, which Khan labels as *authoritarian clientelism*, an intermediate state between *competitive clientelism* and *vulnerable authoritarianism.* Under the present dispensation, the ruling coalition uses organizational restrictions on the opposition but is itself not very consolidated and disciplined. As a result, the configuration is not stable and may drift in different directions.

As is evident, the political and economic institutions, as they exist now in Bangladesh, are far from inclusive. The democracy that prevails is not representative, as it severely limits political competition. Similarly, institutions that provide access to financial resources are not inclusive; individuals' access to these institutions is dependent on one's access to political power—or their political capital—which is highly unequally distributed. This has obvious implications for the economy, particularly for the businesses—which are essentially debt-based, depending exclusively on bank credit. In Bangladesh, the businesses rise and fall with this access to political capital. Companies with strong political connections obtain sweetheart deals whereas those without are capital-starved. When access to financing is based on political capital, it leads to crony capitalism.[10] In addition to its disturbing equity implication, crony capitalism does not lead to enduring growth, as experience suggests.

Demographic Bane[11]

There is a good deal of discussion among policymakers and social scientists about the demographic dividend in Bangladesh as if the benefits are imminent and within grasp. However, many developing countries, including Bangladesh, may not be able to achieve this economic benefit without appropriate policies and substantial investments in human capital. Indeed, as recent development history suggests, the demographic dividend is wasted if such policies and investments are not in place.

The demographic dividend is the surge in economic growth that may result from a decline in a country's mortality and fertility and the subsequent change in the age structure of the population. This decline is often accompanied by an increase in average life expectancy, which increases the size of the working-age population.

Economists have identified four distinct ways the benefits of the demographic dividend can be achieved. The first is the increased labor supply; however, the magnitude of this benefit will depend on the ability of the economy to absorb and productively employ the additional workers. The second is through an increase in savings (resulting from reduced dependency ratio), which, when invested, leads to higher productivity. The third is human capital. Fertility declines result in reduced economic pressures at home, thereby enabling parents to invest more in children's health and education, leading to a healthy and educated labor force. The fourth is the increase in domestic demand resulting from the rise in per capita income and the reduced dependency ratio.

Some of the most compelling evidence of the demographic dividend comes from East Asian countries. Those countries benefitted from the knowledge, experience, and technology of other countries which had already passed through the demographic transition. The Asian Tigers were able to take advantage of the demographic dividend because of their appropriate social and economic policies—including openness to trade and foreign investments, and flexible labor markets—and substantial and continued investments in human capital, including education and public health. About one-third of economic growth between 1965 and 1990 in the East Asian countries is attributed to their demographic dividend (Asian Development Bank 1997).

To reap the benefit of the demographic dividend, it is important to make strategic investments in health and education, areas where Bangladesh has underinvested in the past. It is reflected in the World Bank's recently launched "human capital" index, which scores country investments in health and education. This index reflects whether the health and education systems lead to a productive workforce that can face the dynamic nature of work as technology begins to change. Although the human capital ranking is dominated by Asian countries such as Singapore, Korea, Hong Kong, and Japan, South Asia including Bangladesh fares badly. Of the 157 countries rated, Bangladesh ranked 106 with a score of 0.48, which is below the World Average (see Table 4.3). The quality of schools was found to be abysmal. Although a child who now starts school at 4 can expect to complete 11 years of schooling by his or her 18th birthday, factoring in what children can learn, the expected years of education amount to only 6.5 years (World Bank 2018).

In addition to the quality of the workforce, the country suffers from serious under- and unemployment issues. In Bangladesh, between 2000 and 2010, the total working-age population and the total labor force each

Table 4.3 Human capital scores and indexes of selected countries—2018

Country	*Score*	*Rank*
Bangladesh	0.48	106
India	0.44	115
Nepal	0.49	102
Pakistan	0.39	134
Cambodia	0.49	100
Vietnam	0.67	48

Source: World Bank (2018)

Note: Scores are on a scale of 0 to 1 and based on how many children survive to school age and to adulthood without stunted growth and how much they learn at school

increased by about 2 million annually. However, total employment grew by only 1.5 million annually. Most of the increase is in the informal sector due to the relatively limited number of jobs created in the formal sector. The employment structure of Bangladesh is characterized by the predominance of the low-productivity, low-wage, informal sector, which cannot contribute much to poverty reduction. Like many developing countries, the official unemployment rate is quite low (around 4.0 percent) (Bangladesh Bureau of Statistics (BBS) 2017); however, it conceals a considerable volume of underemployment, differently estimated at between 17 and 34 percent, which is of greater concern. The situation is even more precarious when it comes to the employment of college and university graduates. According to an estimate by the Economist Intelligence Unit (2014), the percentage of secondary school graduates enrolled in tertiary education has more than doubled between 2004 and 2011. However, this increase has not been accompanied by an adequate increase in employment for university graduates. Of these graduates, about 47 percent were without jobs in 2012. There are many reasons for this increasing unemployment rate for the most educated of the labor force. Besides the low quality of education, there are serious mismatches between demand and supply of skills. If the economy cannot significantly enhance its employment-generating capacity, the ranks of unemployed and underemployed will soon reach even more alarming levels.

However, the crux of the problem is that while the service sector is creating jobs, these are relatively low-productivity jobs. As a result, per capita income in Bangladesh has not benefited as much from the intersectoral migration of workers out of agriculture as in many Southeast and East Asian countries. Moving forward, Bangladesh's challenge will be to create the conditions for faster growth of productive jobs in manufacturing and the formal service sector. In the absence of such job growth, the demographic dividend could turn into a demographic nightmare.

A demographic bulge is a double-edged sword. If demography is harnessed correctly, it can yield higher savings, higher investments, and higher growth. If it is not managed well, it can lead to higher unemployment, lower savings, lower investments, and lower growth. Moreover, and finally, in the context of a weak state, the demographic bulge can be the stuff of social revolutions. A case in point is the Arab Spring. While a whole range of countries from India to the Middle East to sub-Saharan Africa are presumably poised to reap demographic dividends, few have succeeded in translating this dividend into fast growth; on the contrary, this army of unemployed youth could be that powder keg to ignite social explosions, as illustrated by the 2010 Arab Spring (Lin 2012).

Demography can be a serious challenge for Bangladesh if there is a slowdown in the current pace of growth.

Dwindling Social Capital

Harvard political science professor Robert Putnam defines social capital as "connections among individuals – social networks and norms of reciprocity and trustworthiness that arise from them" (Putnam 2000, 18). Simply stated, social capital is the glue that holds society together. This bond, when it exists, fosters reciprocity, cooperation, and trust among members of society. Quantitative data as well as case studies suggest that social capital—by fostering cooperation and trust between individuals—facilitates collective action for the common good and promotes economic growth (by, among others, reducing transaction costs and efficiency of markets) (Quibria 2003).

At independence, the society was endowed with an abundance of social capital, based on a common language, culture, ethnicity, and social values, and built on the shared goal of establishing democracy and achieving economic freedom. Over time, things have soured: the economy improved but did not produce a level playing field—while some prospered, others floundered as inequality crept in; democracy became increasingly imperfect and illiberal, and politics became more confrontational and contentious. Economic and social opportunities started to be filtered through the prism of politics. This has set in motion intensely destructive politics, leading to tribalism[12]—political identity began to emerge as the meal ticket to political and economic power. This sentiment of increasing tribalism transformed the whole society into a mosaic of political tribes, where people from one tribe started to view others not only as the opposition but often as mortal enemies. This led to increasingly coarse political rhetoric, declining trust, and dwindling cooperation among groups.

As tribalism metastasized, social capital frayed. There is a good deal of anecdotal evidence to suggest that the country has, in recent years, suffered serious erosion in social capital, though there is no intertemporal data that track the movement of social capital over time.

One set of data that provides a snapshot of social capital across the country is contained in the Legatum Prosperity Index. According to this index, Bangladesh ranks among the lowest, at 133 among 140 countries, in social capital, which is measured in three dimensions: personal and social relationships, the strength of social norms, and the level of civic participation (Legatum Institute 2017). If things do not improve, this crisis of social capital can be a drag on future growth and development.

Leadership Challenge

Though it is recognized that leadership has a critical role to play in economic development, the existing development literature pays scant attention to the role of leadership in the process of economic development (largely because it is difficult to empirically evaluate the impact of leadership on economic growth). There are, however, case studies that starkly illustrate the role of leadership in making and breaking an economy. A case in point is Zimbabwe and Singapore. Both Zimbabwe and Singapore started out with charismatic and durable leaderships in Robert Mugabe and Lee Kwan Yew. While the former brought the economy to a grinding halt, the latter took the economy to soaring heights. With little or no mineral or natural resources, Singapore is a small, insular island whereas Zimbabwe is a country of spectacular waterfalls, places of exquisite natural beauty, and an abundance of natural resources including platinum, gold, and diamond. Starting from an income of less than $500 in 1960, Singapore has now reached a per capita income of almost $60,000, which places it in the ranks of the advanced countries in the world. On the other hand, Zimbabwe also started with an income of less than $500 in 1960, not too far from that of Singapore, but remains mired in poverty—and is yet to cross even the low-income threshold of the World Bank (see Fig. 4.1). Singapore and Zimbabwe provide a study in contrasts with respect to the role of leadership in economic development. As the two previous examples show, much of the prosperity of a nation depends on the quality of its political and economic leadership—and not necessarily on its durability.[13]

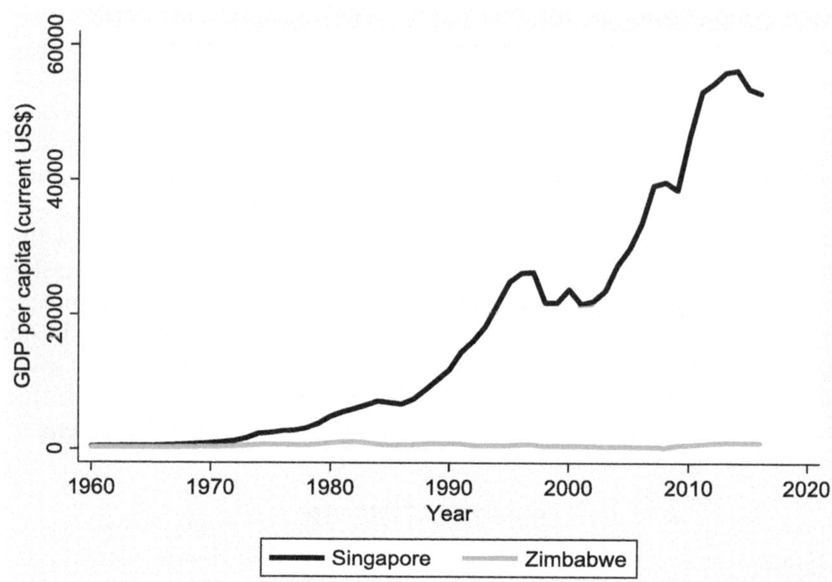

Fig. 4.1 Growth of per capita income of Singapore vis-à-vis Zimbabwe (1960–2016). (Source: World Bank)

According to the Growth Report of the World Bank, the leadership plays a critical role in economic development, which entails (i) devising an appropriate model of growth and development, and policies to sustain it; (ii) creating and sustaining appropriate institutions in support of the model; and finally (iii) managing the politics of growth featuring the ways in which the countries deal with the issues of growth, such as inequality (Brady and Spence 2010).

What is important for the leadership is the cognitive ability to envision a model or devise a strategy—based on the resource constraints, socioeconomic context of the country, as well as the global economic environment—and then build a consensus around it. Even otherwise, great leaders like Mao or Nehru chose an economic model that did not work. In the 1960s, Mao Zedong adopted a strategy of "four modernizations", which entailed the introduction of high-accumulation, low-consumption policies; giving priority to the development of heavy industry; adopting capital-intensive guidelines; and setting highly protective import substitution policies. This strategy, which defied comparative advantage, largely failed (Brady and Spence 2010).

The next step for the leadership is to build coalitions and institutions to sustain politics that allows the plan the time to bring economic dividend to the people. Also, effective leaders should be able to adjust or make course corrections in response to external shocks—such as inequality, shifting comparative advantage, and so on. In a globalized economic environment, a transformative leadership has to combine many abilities, which include a sophisticated understanding of the economy, capacity to articulate an appropriate development model and develop evidence-based policies, master politics and possess problem-solving capacity to course-correct in the face of contingencies. This is a long list of characteristics for a transformative leader, which possibly explains why there are so few such leaders.

Notes

1. World Bank, in its Growth Report, highlights 13 miracle economies that achieved sustained growth rate in the post-World War period, but several of them have yet to reach the status of high-income countries—such as Brazil, Thailand, and Malaysia (World Bank 2008).
2. The middle-income trap is the condition in which a country's growth slows after reaching the middle-income level. Middle-income countries are said to be squeezed between the low-wage poor countries that dominate in mature industries with their low wages and the rich countries that dominate in new industries based on rapid technological change. See Felipe et al. (2014).
3. Mckinsey, in a recent series of reports, has analyzed the impact of automation across countries. The institute suggests that half of human work can be automated by currently demonstrated technology. However, it notes that the pace and extent of automation would be determined by the ongoing development of technological capabilities, the cost of technology, competition with labor including skills, and supply and demand dynamics (Mckinsey Global Institute 2017; Mckinsey Global Institute 2015).
4. This section draws extensively from USAID (2015) and Government of Bangladesh and FAO (2011), which use data from many different sources such as the Ministry of Agriculture; Food and Agricultural Organization; World Food Program; Food Planning and Monitoring Unit; and the Ministry of Disaster Management and relief. Unless otherwise stated, data in this section are drawn from these sources, as cited in the reports.
5. The reason for this imbalance in the use of fertilizer is that poor farmers are often unable to procure and apply balanced inputs for crop production. In addition, farmers no longer use crop residue and cow dung for enriching the soil. These days, crop residues are increasingly being used for households, rather than leaving them in the field as compost; and cow dung is mostly used as fuel, rather than fertilizer (Government of Bangladesh and FAO 2011).

6. A moral hazard issue exists here: There is an expectation that if a state-owned bank becomes insolvent or a large part of the assets goes bad, the government would bail out the bank and inject new capital.
7. Transparency International has produced a *Corruption Perceptions Index* (CPI) since 1995. The CPI views corruption as the abuse of public power for private benefit. Since 2012, the CPI has ranked 176 countries "on a scale from 100 (very clean) to 0 (highly corrupt)". In prior years, the scale ran from 10 to 0. The 2012 CPI draws on 13 different surveys and assessments from 12 different institutions. The 13 surveys/assessments are either opinion surveys of business people or performance assessments from risk agencies and international organizations (Quibria 2015).
8. The WGI dataset—which is based on the polls of experts and surveys of businesspeople and general citizens—is an amalgam of governance data from a wide variety of sources. The WGI compile and summarize information from 30-plus data sources of four different types: (i) surveys of households and firms (nine data sources, including the Afrobarometer surveys, Gallup World Poll, and Global Competitiveness Report survey); (ii) commercial business information providers (four data sources, including the Economist Intelligence Unit, Global Insight, Political Risk Services); (iii) nongovernmental organizations (nine data sources, including Global Integrity, Freedom House, Reporters Without Borders); and (iv) public sector organizations (eight data sources, including the CPIA assessments of World Bank and regional development banks, the EBRD Transition Report, French Ministry of Finance Institutional Profiles Database).
9. In his *Politics as a Vocation*, Max Weber argued that a nation-state can be defined by its monopoly over legitimate use of violence against residents of its territory. However, this monopoly must be acquired through a process of legitimation (Weber 1946).
10. Citing the *Daily Star*, Khan (2017) noted that in 2014, Beximco, one of the politically connected business groups asked for a rescheduling of its nonperforming loans, amounting to $700 million. Restructuring of $130 million was immediately granted by Sonali Bank and $240 million by Janata Bank. Not only was Beximco granted a two-year grace period but also 2–3 percent interest rate reduction. Another nine politically connected business groups were also granted loan-rescheduling equivalent to $1.8 billion.
11. This draws on Barkat-e-Khuda and Quibria (2015).
12. Political tribalism does not have to be based on ethnic fragmentation.

    For a recent book on political tribalism in the United States, see Chua (2018) who describes how American society has become increasingly fragmented into tribes, and its democracy into "an engine of zero-sum tribalism".
13. Durability is a double-edge sword. In a good leader, it represents continuity and credibility of policies, leading to a virtuous cycle of higher savings,

higher investments, and higher growth. In a bad leader, it may mean perpetuation of bad policies, wastage of resources (both natural and fiscal), leading to a spiral of corruption and cronyism and economic stagnation—or, even worse, economic decline. An interesting short account on the decline of Zimbabwe is found in Power (2003).

References

Acemglou, D., and J.A. Robinson. 2013. *Why Nations Fail: The Origins of Power, Prosperity and Poverty*. New York: Crown Publishing Group.

Anner, Mark. 2018. *The Sourcing Squeeze: Workers' Rights and Building Safety in Bangladesh Since Rana Plaza*. Research Report. University Park: Center for Global Workers' Rights, Penn State University.

Asian Development Bank. 1997. *Emerging Asia: Changes and Challenges*. Manila: Asian Development Bank.

———. 2017. *Meeting Asia's Infrastructure Need*. 50th Anniversary Publication. Manila: ADB.

Bangladesh Bureau of Statistics (BBS). 2017. *Quarterly Labor Force Survey 2015–16*. Dhaka: BBS.

Barkat-e-Khuda, and M.G. Quibria. 2015. Reaping Demographic Dividend. *The Daily Star*. March 08. https://www.thedailystar.net/reaping-demographic-dividend-18430. Accessed 27 Oct 2018.

BBC (British Broadcasting Corporation). 2012. *Bangladesh Rail Minister Resigns in Corruption Scandal*. April 12. Accessed 1 Oct 2018.

Brady, David, and Michael Spence. 2010. *Leadership and Politics: A Perspective from the Commission on Growth and Development*, 1–17. Washington, DC: World Bank. https://openknowledge.worldbank.org/handle/10986/2404

Chua, Amy. 2018. *Political Tribes: Group Instinct and the Fate of Nations*. New York: Penguin Random House.

Daily Mail. 2018. Saudis Are Forced to Work as Mechanics, Tea-Sellers and Burger Flippers for the First Time as Austerity Bites. July 31. https://www.dailymail.co.uk/news/article-6013627/Burger-wheels-Saudis-try-lowly-jobs-economy-bites.html. Accessed 29 Sept 2018.

Dhaka Tribune. 2018. NCPSSR: Road Accidents Killed 4284 People in 2017. January 2. https://www.dhakatribune.com/bangladesh/2018/01/01/ncpsrr-road-accidents-2017. Accessed 6 Oct 2018.

Fan, Qimiao, and Martin Rama. 2017. Seize the Opportunity Now to Make Dhaka a Great Modern City. *The Daily Star*, July. https://www.thedailystar.net/opinion/society/seize-the-opportunity-make-dhaka-great-modern-city-1435108. Accessed 6 Oct 2018.

Felipe, Jesus, Utsav Kumar, and Reynold Galope. 2014. *Middle Income Transitions: Trap or Myth?* ADB Working Paper Series, No. 421. Manila: Asian Development Bank.

FPMU (Food Policy Monitoring Unit). 2013. *Bangladesh Country Investment Plan*. Dhaka: Food Division, Ministry of Food and Disaster Management.

Government of Bangladesh. 2015. *Seventh Five Year Plan-FY 2016–2020*. Five Year Plan. Dhaka: Bangladesh Planning Commission.

Government of Bangladesh and FAO. 2011. *Towards a Food Secure Bangladesh*. Rome: FAO (Food and Agriculture Organization).

Hallward-Driemeird, Mary, and Gaurav Nayyar. 2018. *Trouble in the Making? The Future of Manufacturing-led Development*. Washington, DC: World Bank.

Hobbs, Michael. 2014. Welcome to the Traffic Capital of the World. *The New Republic*, July 2.

International Labor Organization. 2016. *ASEAN in Transformation: The Future of Jobs at Risk of Automation*. Geneva: International Labor Organization.

International Monetary Fund. 2018. *Saudi Arabia: Selected Issues*. IMF Report No. 18/264, Washington, DC: IMF.

Islam, Nurul. 2014. Overview. In *Ship Adrift: Governance and Development in Bangladesh*, ed. Nurul Islam and Mohammad Asaduzzaman, 11–31. Dhaka: BIDS (Bangladesh Institute of Development Studies).

Khan, Mustaq. 2017. *Anti-corruption in Bangladesh: A Political Settlements Analysis*. Working Paper 003. London: SOAS, University of London.

Legatum Institute. 2017. *The Legatum Prosperity Index 2017*. The Legatum Prosperity Index. London: Legatum Institute.

Lin, Justin. 2012. Youth Bulge: Demographic Dividend or Demographic Bomb in Developing Countries? January 5. http://blogs.worldbank.org/development-talk/youth-bulge-a-demographic-dividend-or-a-demographic-bomb-in-developing-countries. Accessed 29 Oct 2018.

Maplecroft. 2014. *Climate Change and Environment Risk Atlas*. Bath: Verisk Maplecroft. https://www.maplecroft.com/portfolio/new-analysis/2014/10/29/climate-change-and-lack-food-security-multiply-risks-conflict-and-civil-unrest-32-countries-maplecroft/

Mckinsey Global Institute. 2015. *Four Fundamentals of Workplace Automation*. Mckinsey Global Institute.

———. 2017. *A Future that Works: Automation, Employment and Productivity*. Mckinsey Global Institute.

New York Times. 2016. Bangladesh's Other Banking Scam. April 16. https://www.nytimes.com/2016/04/12/opinion/bangladeshs-other-banking-scam.html. Accessed 1 Oct 2018.

Power, Samantha. 2003. How to Kill a Country. *The Atlantic*. https://www.theatlantic.com/magazine/archive/2003/12/how-to-kill-a-country/302845/

Putnam, Robert. 2000. *Bowling Alone*. New York: Simon and Schuster.

Quartz. 2017. *Rise of Sewbots*. August 17. https://qz.com/1064679/a-new-t-shirt-sewing-robot-can-make-as-many-shirts-per-hour-as-17-factory-workers/. Accessed 23 Sept 2018.

Quibria, M.G. 2003. The Puzzle of Social Capital: A Critical Review. *Asian Development Review* 20 (2): 19–40.

———. 2015. Governance in Developing Asia: Concepts, Measurements, Determinant and a Paradox. In *Governance in Developing Asia: Public Service Delivery and Empowerment*, ed. Anil Deolalikar, Shikha Jha, and Pilipinas Quising. London: Edward Elgar.

Rashid, Salim. 2014. Suicidal Land Loss. *Daily Star.* March 15. https://www.thedailystar.net/suicidal-land-loss-16162. Accessed 30 Sept 2018.

Rodrik, Dani. 2016. Premature Deindustrialization. *Journal of Economic Growth* 21: 1–33.

The Daily Star. 2018. Owners Bankrupting Private Banks: Crony Capitalism at Its Worst. September 1. https://www.thedailystar.net/news/editorial/owners-bankrupting-private-banks-1627201. Accessed 1 Oct 2018.

The Economist Intelligence Unit. 2014. *High University Enrolment, Low Graduate Employment.* London: The Economist.

The Wall Street Journal. 2012. World Bank Cancels $1.2 Billion Bangladesh Loan. June 12. https://www.wsj.com/articles/SB10001424052702303561504577498363128959728. Accessed 2 Oct 2018.

———. 2018. The Robots Are Coming for Garment Workers. That's Good for the U.S., Bad for Poor Countries. *The Wall Street Journal.* February 16. https://www.wsj.com/articles/the-robots-are-coming-for-garment-workers-thats-good-for-the-u-s-bad-for-poor-countries-1518797631. Accessed 24 Sept 2018.

Transparency International Bangladesh. 2018. *Corruption in Service Sectors: National Household Survey 2011.* National Household Survey. Dhaka: Transparency International Bangladesh.

UN (United Nations). 2016. *The World Cities in 2016.* New York: United Nations. http://www.un.org/en/development/desa/population/publications/pdf/urbanization/the_worlds_cities_in_2016_data_booklet.pdf

USAID. 2015. *Food Security Country Framework for Bangladesh (Fy 2015–2019).* Washington, DC: USAID.

Weber, Max. 1946. Politics as a Vocation. In *Essays in Sociology*, ed. H.H. Garth and C.W. Mills, 26–45. New York: Macmillan.

World Bank. 2006. *Economics and Governance of Nongovernmental Organizations in Bangladesh.* Bangladesh Development Series, Paper No. 11. Dhaka: The World Bank Office.

———. 2008. *The Growth Report: Strategies for Sustained Growth and Inclusive Development.* Washington, DC: World Bank.

———. 2013. *Enterprise Surveys: Bangladesh 2013.* Washington, DC: World Bank. http://www.enterprisesurveys.org/data/exploreeconomies/2013/bangladesh

———. 2018. *Human Capital Project.* Washington, DC: World Bank. http://www.worldbank.org/en/publication/human-capital

CHAPTER 5

Conclusions

Abstract This chapter strings together the major conclusions of the study. It also provides some observations on political, social, and institutional challenges for the country going forward. These relate to such factors as governance, political institutions, economic openness, industrial policy, labor market and human development policy, investments in physical infrastructure, and the role of leadership.

Keywords Premature deindustrialization • Industrialization 4.0 • Governance and leadership

Pulling the Threads Together

We began the book with a thumbnail sketch of the state of economic development of the country at its founding in 1971. Since then, Bangladesh has made significant strides in economic development, which are reflected in its income growth, reduction in poverty, progress in various social and human indicators, as well as some improvements in infrastructure. In recent years, the country has recorded growth exceeding 7 percent. The county has also advanced to the lower-middle-income group of the World Bank and is on its way to graduate from the least-developed country (LDC) status of the United Nations. Impressive as this progress has been, it would be hasty to conjecture that the future would be a replay of its past performance—and

M. G. Quibria, *Bangladesh's Road to Long-term Economic Prosperity*, https://doi.org/10.1007/978-3-030-11587-6_5

the country will cruise along its current growth trajectory—given the various serious risks and challenges that confront the economy.

It is apparent that much of the recent growth and development has been narrowly based, primarily propelled by what is labeled in this study as the four drivers of development: ready-made garments (RMG); international migration and remittances: agriculture; and nongovernmental organizations (NGOs). While these drivers have served the economy well in the past, their robustness is likely to be challenged in the future. We identify a trifecta of major risks, which are exogenous to the government and largely beyond its ability to manipulate. These are rooted, first, in the rapid changing technology in robotics and artificial intelligence; second, in the evolving global political and economic environment[1]; and third, in climate change and natural disasters.

Of these risks, one relates to the continued viability of labor migration as a strategy of development. The oil-rich economies in the Middle East are currently in a state of political and economic flux. They are increasingly embracing policies of Arabization—substituting foreign workers by nationals—in the face of falling oil prices and increasing domestic unemployment. The Western countries, including European Union countries and the United States, have also seen an upsurge of anti-immigrant sentiments and nativism. Going forward, as these countries transition into the phase of industrialization 4.0, the rate of unemployment will rise—so will negative sentiments toward immigrants. Another class of risk relates to NGOs which have played a significant role in the economic and social transformation of the country. Continuing with this role into the future, these organizations will encounter various internal (structural) as well as external constraints. One important constraint would be funding, as most of these organizations rely heavily on the availability of external grant resources, which would likely witness a gradual waning as the country graduates from its LDC status.

Yet another risk relates to the agriculture sector, which has done a stupendous job of feeding an expanding population, but the future expansion of agricultural productivity will depend on further improvements in seeds, irrigation, and fertilizer technology, which may not be available as required. However, more importantly, much or all the past gains in agricultural productivity may be upended by climate change for which Bangladesh is considered most at risk among all countries in the world. Other than extreme weather conditions such as drought and increased inundation, the country is at risk of experiencing sea-level rise, increased soil erosion, and rising saline contamination. All these may seriously threaten the robustness of the agricultural sector as well as the whole economy. There is no doubt that Bangladesh has been making some investments in climate mitigation and adaption, but they are inadequate in relation to the requirements—the problems are too big for Bangladesh alone to handle!

Apropos agriculture, even though Bangladesh has done a commendable job of controlling fertility, farm size has dwindled rapidly over time owing to land loss from human settlements, urbanization, and road infrastructure, as well as from environmental causes. If the current business-as-usual practice of unrestricted human settlement continues, availability of farmland will diminish exponentially over time. To avert such grim prospects, one requires more regulation as well as innovation in rural housing and land use. While there may be multiple ways of addressing this issue, Salim Rashid has proposed one such model of compact rural township that economizes on land use in housing as well as derives benefits from economies of agglomeration (Rashid 2013).

Finally, perhaps the most important risk relates to technological progress—in particular, the ongoing technological revolution in robotics and artificial intelligence in manufacturing—which threatens to displace workers from labor-intensive manufacturing, such as RMG, and may bring about what has come to be labeled "premature deindustrialization" in newly industrializing nations (Rodrik 2016). This means many developing countries will begin to experience deindustrialization—that is, falling manufacturing shares in output and employment—much before they have attained full industrialization the way advanced countries did.

However, it may be noted that this threat of technology displacing workers is nothing new. Worries about machines eliminating jobs have been around for a long time. As the Industrial Revolution took hold in Britain more than 200 years ago, members of the Luddite movement took sledgehammers to machines in protest at the advent of machines. However, history has proven that Luddites were wrong; machines did not bring wages down or mark the end of work. However, machines have gotten smarter and technologies have been changing. They are substituting unskilled labor and not complementing them. Two leading economists of the United States, Jeffrey Sachs and Lawrence Kotlikoff, mused that horse-drawn coaches of the past were replaced by motorized taxis. However, in both cases, they required a human being with relatively little human-capital investment—a cabbie—to drive them. But tomorrow's cars will drive themselves, picking up, dropping off, and returning home all based on a few keystrokes (or a simple app on a smart phone). This will make cabbies yet another profession of the past (Sachs and Kotlikoff 2012, 1).

They went on to pose a question that is of overarching significance for developing countries as a whole: What if the Luddites are now getting it right, if not for labor as a whole, at least for unskilled labor? Indeed, what happens if machines get so smart, due to their microprocessor brains, that they no longer need unskilled labor to operate? (Sachs and Kotlikoff 2012, 1).

Sachs and Kotlikoff did not answer the question, but Nobel Laureate Wassily Leontief did, a few decades earlier: "The role of humans as the most important factor of production is bound to diminish in the same way that the role of horses … was first diminished and then eliminated" (Leontief 1983, 3).

At the moment, it is unknowable how the risk, associated with this technological change, will pan out over time and affect the manufacturing sector of countries such as Bangladesh. Currently, such automation technology is evolving: it is both expensive and an imperfect substitute for human beings. But as this technology becomes cheaper and more capable, they will increasingly replace human labor in the most routine and repetitive tasks. Technology experts warn that given the current rate of technological progress, it is only a matter of time before automation will outcompete unskilled workers and undermine the economic model that many developing countries have adopted to industrialize.

Nobel Laureate Michael Spence and his coauthors (two leading technology experts) suggest that this trend may extend beyond manufacturing into services:

> Interactive voice response systems, for example, are reducing the requirement for direct person to-person interaction, spelling trouble for call centers in the developing world. Similarly, increasingly reliable computer programs will cut into transcription work now often done in the developing world. In more and more domains, the most cost-effective source of "labor" is becoming intelligent and flexible machines as opposed to low-wage humans in other countries. (Brynjolfsson et al. 2014, 47)

They also opine that the growing capabilities of automation will also undo one of the most reliable strategies that poor countries have used in the past to attract foreign investment by offering low wages to compensate for low productivity and skill levels. And this will apply to foreign direct investment in manufacturing as well as services (Brynjolfsson et al. 2014, 46).

The risks delineated here, either singly or in combination, can slow down or upend the development process by adversely affecting the drivers of development. If they act in unison, the cascading effect will be devastating for the economy.

However, before reaching the point of inflection where large-scale automation starts taking hold on traditionally labor-intensive industries, there will be a transition period when the country can do much to address the challenges that beset its current development process.

Moving Forward

It is well acknowledged that the current growth and export base is narrow—virtually mono-economic around RMG; it needs to further diversify for sustained growth as well as a cushion against faltering development drivers. Such diversification will require addressing various social, political, policy, and institutional challenges facing the economy, including poor governance, inadequate physical infrastructure, skill and educational bottlenecks, demographic burden, dwindling social capital, and lack of transformational leadership. Drawing on our previous discussions of these themes, we offer some general observations on institutions and policies required for the sustained development of the economy.[2]

Poor governance is a luxury a resource-scarce, developing country can hardly afford. If the country seeks to broaden its growth and development, it must clean up various types of corruption and misgovernance. The financial sector is gripped with pervasive mismanagements and shenanigans of enormous magnitudes. The bureaucracy is riddled with inefficiencies and ubiquitous partisanships. The country had a tradition of nonpartisan, meritocratic bureaucracy, a tradition it needs to reclaim. In the allocation of investible funds, the country needs to shun the practice of crony capitalism and must strive for a more competitive system. Also, at a more fundamental level, uncertainty abounds in property rights, contract enforcement, and the rule of law, issues that continue to be a concern for investors, both domestic and foreign.

Good governance—insofar as it ensures property rights, enforces contacts, and provides transparency of government regulation and credible policy—has been a magnet for attracting foreign investment. It is therefore hard to overstate the importance of good governance—it is not only a direct contributor to citizens' welfare but also, in many ways, a potent instrument of economic development.

The lesson of history is that it is difficult to get the economics right without getting the politics right (Acemglou and Robinson 2013). Under the current dispensation, political power is highly concentrated, and the current system is neither inclusive nor contested. Politics is highly contentious and confrontational. There is an uneasy sense of political stability, based not on democratic consensus but on political machination. An analyst aptly described the current state of political stability as "more order but less law". Durable political stability, which can only be achieved through pluralistic, participatory democracy, will be essential to sustain future development.

By all indicators, Bangladesh has invested poorly in infrastructure, compared to many other Asian neighbors. The pace of future development of the country will depend on its ability to make the required investments and execute them with efficiency and probity. It needs to invest in its roads and highways, ports, electricity, telecommunications, and its cities like Dhaka and Chittagong. Dhaka, once one of the greatest cities in the world, is in its death throes. To make it more functional and more habitable, it would require substantial investments in its infrastructure, as well as measures toward decentralization (both administrative and fiscal). Although the government has over the years taken some baby steps toward decentralization, it is still one of the most centralized countries in the world—with everything orbiting around Dhaka.

There is no policy that carries such universal approval as investments in human capital. The country needs to scale up its investments at all levels of education. If Bangladesh wants to be globally competitive through trade either in manufacturing or in services, it needs to provide its younger generation more and better (quality) education that fosters creativity and seeds innovation, the lifeblood of a modern dynamic economy. With digitization, the global labor market is becoming more integrated, opening up new opportunities for trade in services where competitiveness is determined mainly by the quality of education and infrastructure.

The country is currently experiencing a potential demographic dividend—a bulge in the working-age population due to demographic transition. There is nothing automatic about demographic dividend. This dividend needs to be harnessed by creating well-paid jobs in manufacturing and services; otherwise, it could turn into a demographic nightmare, more so in this age of rapidly changing technology.

If there is a common trait that runs among of the East Asian miracle economies as well as such unfolding miracles as Vietnam, it is their outward orientation—openness to trade and investment. This openness allowed these economies to tap into the virtually unlimited international trading opportunities in the world economy and to access new technology (Quibria 2002). Bangladesh needs to improve its trading regime by accelerating its stalled tariff reform (to be worked in conjunction with domestic indirect taxes); whatever openness it achieved in its outward orientation, much of it has been annulled by the ad hoc imposition of para-tariffs, which benefits neither the consumers nor the producers. Along with trade liberalization (achieved either unilaterally or through free-trade agreements), the country also needs to maintain for its sustained economic growth a stable and competitive real exchange rate. However, going forward, the country is likely to encounter less generous trading regimes abroad. As the country graduates from its LDC status, it would experience an erosion of trade preferences in the form of duty-free access to the European Union and other countries such as Canada, as well as the loss of WTO's Trade-Related Aspects of Intellectual Property Rights waiver for LDC pharmaceuticals for production and export of drugs. All this will have an adverse impact on Bangladesh's trade and GDP.

With respect to foreign investment, there are many obstacles, including corruption, political uncertainty, transparency of the regulatory regime, and scarcity of land, as captured by the World Bank's Ease of Doing Business, where Bangladesh ranks 177 out of 190 countries (World Bank 2018).

To promote export and broaden the base of the economy, one suggested route is the industrial policy which takes many forms including regulatory reform, tax breaks, subsidies, and tariffs up to the bound-rate. However, it may be noted that Post-War economic history is littered with the corpses of failed industrial policy (because it is difficult to pick winners and losers). However, there are some arguably successful instances, including Japan and Korea. Therefore, such policies should be cautiously approached. Nobel Laureate Jean Tirole proposed a few guidelines for such policy such as identify the reason for the market failure; in order to respond effectively, use appropriately qualified experts to select industries; adopt a neutral industrial policy that does not distort competition between companies; include a "sunset-clause" which ensures that support can be withdrawn if the policy is not working or is no longer needed (Tirole 2017).

The labor market situation in Bangladesh, which is more flexible—meaning more deregulated—than India's, has been friendlier to manufacturing growth. Yet, at the same time, the country has a large potential workforce (aged 15 and above) exceeding 106 million, a significant portion of which are under- or unemployed. In a populous country of this size, it is extremely important for economic and social stability that workers receive a fair share of output as real wage, commensurate with their contributions to production. Maintaining a balance between labor-market flexibility and a fair wage reflecting the workers' contribution to output is important to ensure inclusive growth, firm profitability, industrial peace, and stability in the face of macroeconomic shocks. Going forward, the government needs to pay attention to this balance.

Bangladesh is experiencing a rising trend in inequality and relative deprivation, which might get worse in the future because of the cascading effects of technology, global economic environment, and climate change among others. For social and political stability, it will be essential that the future growth process be more inclusive. And this will require expanding economic opportunities for the economically less-privileged segments of the society through investments in pro-poor physical and social infrastructure, good governance, and capacity building, as well as creating improved access to education, finance, and sanitation.

Finally, the task of leadership in a developing country is complex and will become increasingly so with the currently unfolding technological revolution (industry 4.0) and the fluid state of globalization. Leadership involves not only managing politics but also dealing with economics in all its complexities—including designing reforms in institutions and policies to address the evolving binding constraints to growth and making course corrections in the face of external or internal shocks. Managing politics can only provide the durability of a regime, but it does not necessarily ensure a country's economic success. Economic success requires that leaders have a sophisticated understanding of the economy and the ability to devise a growth model or strategy for the future. The leadership can be helped in this effort by an efficient and meritocratic bureaucracy (as well as thinks tanks and universities). The East Asian miracle economies provide examples of such bureaucracies—as well as such technocratic organizations as the Economic Planning Bureau in Korea and the Industrial Development Bureau in Taipei, China, which were autonomous of the rough and tumble of quotidian politics and were entrusted with the task of formulating development policies and guiding their implementation.

This provides an outline of an agenda for reform. Given the specter of various risks facing the economy, the tasks ahead are both urgent and challenging. The current growth and export base is highly concentrated; while the old drivers of growth and development are gradually wearing out, there are no obvious new drivers of growth in sight. In these circumstances, there is a crying need for a body of deep-seated reforms, encompassing both economics and politics of the country, as outlined earlier. An important question is the following: Can the leadership rise to the task? If the leadership stumbles, the long-term development consequences can be dire. However, if it succeeds, it can hope not only to add new drivers of development and diversify the economy, but also to mitigate some of the adverse consequences of long-term risks.

Notes

1. The current international environment is in a tumultuous state. It is fraught with many challenges relating to rising trade frictions between nations; weakening of the multilateral institutions regulating global trade; increasing geopolitical conflicts, leading to a rising volume of displaced persons seeking asylum; and growing volatility in oil prices.
2. However, we desist from making any attempt at providing detailed blueprints of such institutions and policies. While those blueprints are instructive, they cannot be cherry-picked and transplanted verbatim in other contexts. In addition, part of the process involves adaptation, sequencing, and pragmatism, what President Deng Xiaoping famously summarized as "crossing the river by feeling the stones".

References

Acemglou, D., and J.A. Robinson. 2013. *Why Nations Fail: The Origins of Power, Prosperity and Poverty*. New York: Crown Publishing Group.

Brynjolfsson, Eric, Andrew McAfee, and Michael Spence. 2014. New World Order. *Foreign Affairs*: 44–53, July–August.

Leontief, Wassily. 1983. The Definition of Problem and Opportunity. In *The Long-term Impact of Technology in Employment and Unemployment*, by National Academy of Engineering, 3–8. New York: National Academy of Engineering.

Quibria, M.G. 2002. *Growth and Poverty: Lessons from the East Asian Miracle Revisited*. Research Paper Series, No: 33. Tokyo: Asian Development Institute.

Rashid, Salim. 2013. *Compact Townships and the Magical 10%*. Dhaka: The University Press.

Rodrik, Dani. 2016. Premature Deindustrialization. *Journal of Economic Growth* 21 (1): 1–33.

Sachs, Jeffrey, and Lawrence Kotlikoff. 2012. *Smart Machines and Long-term Misery*. NBER Working Paper Series 2–19.

Tirole, Jean. 2017. *Economics for the Common Good*. Princeton: Princeton University Press.

World Bank. 2018. *Doing Business*. Business Report. Washington, DC: World Bank.

Index[1]

[1]Note: Page numbers followed by 'n' refer to notes.

M. G. Quibria, *Bangladesh's Road to Long-term Economic Prosperity*, https://doi.org/10.1007/978-3-030-11587-6

The manufacturer's authorised representative in the EU is Springer
Nature Customer Service Centre GmbH, Europaplatz 3, 69115 Heidelberg,
Germany. If you have any concerns regarding our products, please
contact ProductSafety@springernature.com

Printed and bound by CPI Group (UK) Ltd, Croydon, CR0 4YY
22/09/2026
02221067-0016